Free Range Farm Girl

COOKING GRASSFED BEEF

HEALTHY RECIPES FROM NOSE TO TAIL

SHANNON HAYES

A Publication of LEFT TO WRITE PRESS

Also available from Shannon Hayes

Long Way on a Little: An Earth Lover's Companion for Enjoying Meat, Pinching Pennies and Living Deliciously

Radical Homemakers: Reclaiming Domesticity from a Consumer Culture

The Farmer and the Grill

The Grassfed Gourmet

Available at www.ShannonHayes.org and www.GrassfedCooking.com, as well as through most conventional booksellers.

E-Book
ISBN 978-0-9794391-5-5
Print on demand
ISBN 978-0-9794391-7-9
Library of Congress Control Number: 2014943197

Cover and interior design and production: Jill Shaffer
Cover and interior illustrations: © 2012 Jill Webber
E-book Design: David Wogahn, Sellbox
Editor: Bob Hooper

Left to Write Press
270 Rossman Valley Rd
Richmondville, NY 12149
www.ShannonHayes.org
www.GrassfedCooking.com
518.827.7595

About Left to Write Press

Left to Write Press is an initiative of Shannon Hayes and Bob Hooper, who wanted to publish books completely on their own terms, so they could earn a decent return on Shannon's writing without selling their souls. We are now on our fifth book, and we've managed to stick to our guns. Left to Write Press expresses our agenda for an ecologically sound, socially just world, where everyone is well-fed and happy. Now stop reading this small print, and start enjoying our book!

For my blog readers,
who fuel my fire, stir the pot,
and keep me cooking.

Contents

CHAPTER EIGHT: *Beef Seasonings, Rubs, Pastes, and Marinades*   101

Introduction

I'm a home cook, not a professional chef. However, my years of training about quality meat have been just as extensive, if not more so. They began with a childhood spent on the land that I still walk today, where I scrambled along the rocky ledges and wandered the hills of my family's farm, helped my neighbors string fence, make hay and fix barns, and watched as my father butchered livestock in the barnyard. I developed an awareness of the seasons and their impact upon our livestock, which I sensed as I tasted the fruits of my family's labor and the gifts of our animals on my daily plate. Having grown up enjoying good food, my palate has learned to discern when an animal has had a good life, and when it hasn't. As I've come into my family's grassfed meat business, I've stood in our cutting room for hours on end, breathing in the scent of dry-aged beef as the cool steaks slip between my fingers, as I slice the waxy suet for the rendering pot, and pat kabobs into place onto trays. As I hold that beef in my hands, I can see and feel the effects of the well-managed pastures that nourished the animal; when I grab a piece off the table to cook for my lunch, I will taste these benefits as well.

Thus, after publishing several cookbooks on the subject, I've come to believe that the most essential ingredient when preparing a piece of meat is an understanding of how the animal lived, and how it died. If you are hoping for a book that politely separates the pretty cattle in the pasture from the food on your plate, you'd probably better find some glossy armchair cookbook to read. Life and death are forever in service to each other, and when we sit down to a meal, it tastes a whole lot better when we know that the life given up for our sustenance was a happy one, lived in harmony with the earth. When we have a fuller understanding of that life, we'll have a much easier time fixing a tasty supper, as our inner spirits guide us to learn to use the animal's gifts with prudence and gratitude, enabling plentitude for all.

In the following pages, I'll review the basics about what grassfed beef is and its many benefits. Then I'll discuss how to make sense of all the different cuts available at a typical farmers' market, or that you might find in your boxes if you order a side of local grassfed beef for your freezer. We'll learn how the animal's basic anatomy (which determines the cuts) guides our choice of cooking method, and how the fact that the beef has been grassfed (and *not* grainfed) will affect the cooking techniques. After that, we'll launch into recipes making use of those methods, beginning with the fundamental ingredients of bones and fat, then moving on to pan-frying and oven roasting; then braises, soups, and stews; followed by a chapter on grilling and barbecue; a chapter dedicated exclusively to ground beef; and finally, a chapter outlining basic seasonings for dry rubs, pastes, marinades and barbecue sauces. By the end, you should be able to cook everything from the tongue to the tail with ease and confidence.

Whether you hold a degree in culinary arts, or you are just beginning to transition from frozen TV dinners to a real food diet, I promise you will come away from this book knowing a lot more about the food you eat, and how to make it taste more delicious than you ever imagined. It all begins with an understanding of what makes good beef.

CHAPTER ONE
Grassfed Basics

As the western world awakens to the importance of making good food choices, beef consumers are inundated with a tangle of new vocabulary that describes their meat. This book deals exclusively with cooking *grassfed* beef, but before I explain too much more about it, let's clarify some of the other terms that you might hear used to describe the meat you are buying.

Free-range. The *free-range* label implies that animals had *access* to an outdoor area. While some farmers and much of the American public use the term to describe *grass-fed* meats, technically this term does not mean the livestock were raised on pasture, or that grass was included in their diet (although it may have been).

Pasture-raised or pastured. Pasture-raised animals are raised on pastures, of course, and the moniker includes meat and dairy products from ruminants (animals that thrive eating only grass) like sheep, cows, buffalo and goats. However, unlike "grassfed," the term also applies to products from omnivorous critters, like pigs and chickens. Omnivores need additional protein in their diets, which is typically fed as grains containing soy or fish meal. While they cannot subsist on grass alone, they will happily graze in pasture, where they can also satisfy a portion of their protein requirement as they hunt about for bugs, worms and such. So, while all grassfed animals are pastured, not all pastured animals are grassfed. Grassfed livestock receive no grain. Pasture-raised animals do. On our farm, we differentiate by labeling our products, "Grassfed Lamb and Beef" and "Pasture-Raised Pork and Poultry."

Grassfed. In October 2007, the US Department of Agriculture officially defined *grassfed* as *meat that comes from animals whose diet, with the exception of milk consumed prior to weaning, is derived solely from forage (grasses, forbs, cereal crops in the pre-grain state, and browse).*

According to the USDA, animals must have continuous access to pasture during the growing season. Hay, haylage, baleage, silage, non-grain crop residue and other roughage sources are also acceptable feed sources. This is a "voluntary standard" for production, wherein livestock producers have the option of requesting official USDA verification of their grassfed claims. This definition has stirred some controversy among farmers in the movement, and some organizations are working to come up with a new, more strict, definition of *grassfed* and to have an inspection and certification program similar to what has been adopted by the organic industry.

In my personal opinion, while these labels are meant to help consumers better understand how their meat was produced, they can be very confusing. Adding to the confusion, some also use the term "grass-*finished*," which can imply either that the animal was grain-fed when young, but "finished" (brought to market weight and condition) on grass; *or* it might imply that the animal has been grassfed for it's entire life, including the final weeks of "finishing." Truly, with all this terminology, the best way to know if you are getting good meat is to visit the farm, look your farmer in the eye, and ask to see how the animals are raised. A good grazier is generally proud to show you. If that isn't possible, spend some time getting acquainted with the farmer or vendor selling meats at your weekly market, and ask questions. The key point to determine is that the animals are eating grass for their entire lives; either from grazing, or from stored grass crops such as hay. You want to make sure that the beef animals *never* receive grain. Why is that? I'm so glad you asked . . .

THE GRASSFED DIFFERENCE

Recently, there is an emerging, almost instinctive awareness that buying locally produced foods from small-scale family farms is "the right thing to do." While the new "locavore" movement is becoming part of the contemporary zeitgeist, there are a number of very real reasons that grassfed meats are (and always have been) better for your health, our environment, our communities, and animal welfare.

Environmental Benefits. Any of us who love a good juicy burger has endured the finger-wagging of a zealous environmentalist vegetarian who tells us that our meat consumption is not only cruel, but causing the planet to cook, and that our culinary habits are going to cause the oceans to swell, and the weather to get crazy. This notion was fueled by a 2006 report by the UN Food and Agriculture Organization, which claimed that livestock production is responsible for more greenhouse gas emissions than all forms of transportation combined. Though the study that led to this pronouncement was quickly de-bunked, and the UN later released a revised study retracting these strident claims, few people are aware of these corrections, because the "meat is bad" message had already penetrated the media (to learn more on this topic, see my comprehensive book on cooking all grassfed and pastured meats, Long Way on a Little).

In truth, some meat *is* bad—*really, really* bad. If your meat has come from a feedlot (which describes virtually all conventional grocery store beef), the cattle you are eating have been fed a steady diet of grain while confined in some pretty squalid conditions. The horrific practices now known as "factory farming" have been thoroughly described in countless reports and exposés, but here's the bottom line: Feedlot beef requires that massive amounts of grain be grown, cultivated, fertilized, sprayed with pesticides, fungicides, and herbicides, irrigated, mechanically harvested, processed, and then trucked all over the nation (even across the planet) before it is fed to thousands, even hundreds of thousands of animals all standing in cramped corrals, up to their hocks in manure and mud. The animals are then trucked from these feedlots to slaughterhouses hundreds or thousands of miles away, where they are processed with countless other animals from equally squalid settings before the product is trucked another few thousand miles to your local store—the one with the pretty picture of the happy cow over the meat counter. Aside from the dubious wholesomeness of the meat, all of these practices required massive amounts of fossil fuels for monoculture cropping; transport; large amounts of antibiotic and medications to combat the toxicity of the feedlots; and they generate lots of runoff and atmospheric pollution along the way.

But grassfed meat is different.

Foremost, we grass farmers have figured out something pretty cool about our livestock: they have legs, which means that they can roam and forage for their food, rather than having to stand still in a feedlot and have their food trucked to them. When they are allowed to graze, their growth and well-being are not reliant on fossil fuels. These magnificent animals magically convert the simple ingredients of sunshine and water into food, requiring virtually no fossil fuels. In properly managed pastures, the action of their hooves on the pasture helps to improve the quality of the soil, and the gift of their droppings continually restores the fertility of the land. Good grazing stimulates the diversification of plant species and habitat, and extends the seasonal productivity of our pastures (which increases the availability of local food). Better still, studies have shown that with good grazing practices, pastures become excellent "carbon sinks" that are able to pull excess climate-changing carbon dioxide from the atmosphere, and fix it into the soil. That's an outstanding accomplishment for that simple grassfed burger on your plate.

Economic Benefits. I know . . . it can be hard to believe that there is an economic advantage to grassfed meat when each cut costs 15%-50% more than the factory-farmed meat. The truth is that, through tax-funded agricultural subsidies that largely support ecologically devastating grain-based farming, you've paid just as much for the grainfed beef. These subsidies hide the true costs of factory-farmed foods, which makes them *appear* to be cheaper in the grocery store. We're also paying other hidden costs of factory-farmed meat through polluted water, nitrous oxide and carbon emissions, and excessive use of fossil fuels. Grass-based farmers typically qualify for none of these Farm Bill subsidies. Thus, we price our products according to their true costs of production. We're asking for a living wage to produce it for you. In exchange, we are able to be contributing members to our local economies, support numerous other service-related businesses, pay our property taxes and keep the land in your bioregion vibrant and productive. Further, while you may be paying a little bit more for your food, you'll probably be paying a lot less in medical expenses, owing to its health benefits.

The Health Benefits of Grassfed Meat and Dairy Products. Grassfed meats are a good source of Omega-3 fatty acids, which are essential to healthy heart and brain function, and which have been shown to slow the growth of a number of cancers. The meat and dairy products from grassfed animals are also a source of conjugated linoleic acids, or CLAs, another critical nutrient for battling and preventing cancer. In fact, grassfed meat and dairy products are shown to be three to five times higher in CLAs than conventional meat and dairy. An added bonus is that grassfed meats are also significantly higher in Vitamin E than other conventionally grown products. Vitamin E, a nutrient deficient in many Americans, is an important antioxidant that also helps with hormone regulation and supports heart, respiratory, brain, prostate and breast health. All of this is assuming the beef is 100 percent grassfed; even if an animal is raised on grass most of its life, but is then given grain to "fatten up" the last few weeks of life, these nutritional benefits vanish.

When we make an effort to expand our culinary repertoire to include bone broth, rendered animal fats and grassfed organ meats (which you will learn in the coming pages), the nutritional bonuses keep coming. Bone broth is a great source of proteinaceous gelatin and electrolytes, and the fats and organ meats are important sources of the fat-soluble vitamins essential to our health: A, D, E, and K, all which are critical to our body's ability to absorb the other nutrients it requires. The great news about grassfed products is always growing. To learn more about the most up-to-date health findings, be sure to visit eatwild.com, a comprehensive web resource devoted to disseminating the good news about going grassfed.

The best news of all, however, is the fact that the meat just tastes wonderful. Admittedly, that's not the experience everyone has had. Since launching GrassfedCooking.com, I've received a number of letters from readers who have had lousy grassfed dinners. When we begin trouble-shooting, however, I almost always learn that the beef was fine—the mistake was made in the kitchen. So let's talk about how to cook grassfed beef successfully.

CHAPTER TWO
How to Cook Grassfed

While the forthcoming pages offer dozens of recipes, you'll have a much better time working through them if you first learn the basic principles for cooking grassfed meats. Once you understand their culinary differences, you'll have an easier time selecting appropriate recipes. Better still, even if you don't have this cookbook on hand, if you understand these few principles, you should be able to "wing it," coming up with your own fabulous dishes on the spot, based on what looked good at the market, or what was on top of the freezer beef pile.

To cook grassfed beef successfully, it is helpful to first understand the criteria by which most of us unknowingly evaluate meat palatability: juiciness, flavor, and tenderness.

Juiciness. On occasion, I've had customers approach me at my market after buying a piece of meat, complaining that it was dry. Rather than reimbursing their money, I give them a copy of one of my cookbooks. The juiciness of a piece of meat is completely in control of the cook; the farmer and the butcher have no control over whether your chops or roasts are dry. Rather, it is prolonged exposure to high heat that causes the muscle fibers to contract and squeeze the juice out of meat; to avoid this, lower the flame. Be aware that once meat crosses an internal temperature of 145 degrees Fahrenheit, the muscle fibers contract at an accelerated rate, drying the meat out super fast. If you are working with meat that might be lean (grassfed meat may be lean or fatty, depending on myriad variables), lower the heat.

Flavor. Okay, prepare yourself for a bit of a rant . . . Flavor sensitivity has been largely obliterated from the American palate. Most Americans, accustomed to eating lots of processed foods, can discern little more than sweet, sour or salty. Often they are simply unable to detect the nuances of genuine flavor or, if they do, they may find the experience alienating. Hence, most Americans seem more fixated on the texture and tenderness of a cut of meat, rather than the overall taste.

Grassfed beef flavors are more assertive. The "beefiness" is largely a result of the dry-aging process most grass-farmers use, and the meat has the added dimension of a mineral flavor profile and a sweet herbaceousness that can come only from animals who've feasted on nutrient-rich pastures. Grain-fed beef tends to have a flat, indistinct, almost nonexistent taste. When we ran blind taste tests with factory-farmed meat in our home kitchen, we discovered that we couldn't differentiate between factory-farmed beef, lamb and pork. The shortcut "wet-aging" process used in conventional meat production probably has a lot to do with this, because it allows no concentration of the inherent species-specific flavor of the different meats. Moreover, the distinctive mineral-herby taste that comes from the pastures was also missing from the flavor profile.

Often, the person who does have a well-developed palate will find that grassfed meat is the *only* acceptable meat. Factory-farmed meat simply tastes repugnant to them. Beyond mere personal preferences, I believe this is an important consideration as we seek to create a more sustainable world for our children: if we help them cultivate an acute sense of taste, I believe that they will instinctively make food choices that are most beneficial for our planet.

Tenderness. My frequent diatribes about flavor notwithstanding, most Americans consider tenderness to be the most important factor in determining meat palatability. In the meat industry, tenderness is evaluated using a Warner-Bratzler scale, which calculates a tenderness score based on a shear force value. Basically, the tenderness score, reported either in pounds or kilograms, is the amount of force required to tear a half-inch core of a meat sample. The lower the score, the more tender the meat.

Researchers at Texas A & M University found that if beef loin samples (one of the most tender primals) had shear values of seven pounds, they could be 95 percent confident that consumers would find their steaks to be "slightly tender." At Cornell University, I ran some tenderness tests with meat scientist Denny Shaw, using top round roasts, cuts that came from one of the *less* tender primals on the beef. We compared shear tests on wet-aged, factory-farmed certified Angus rounds to dry-aged grassfed rounds. The average score for the factory-farmed beef was 6.27 pounds. The average score for the grassfed beef was 5.20 pounds. The grassfed was more tender every time.

How could this be, when grassfed has the reputation of being tougher? The answer is simple: all of the tenderness and production factors that determine the meat quality were properly addressed. On the farm, the animals and pastures were well handled. The harvest was gentle and quiet; the carcasses were dry-aged. And, finally, the cook (yes, I cooked it) handled the meat properly.

And what is "proper" when it comes to grassfed meat cooking, you ask? Excellent question. Indeed, you have an entire volume before you on just this subject, plus my other cookbooks! However, despite the hundreds of recipes covering that content, there are really only three rules you need to remember:

1. Use lower flames. Lower flames (or oven temperatures) help to hold juice in a piece of meat, as they slow the contraction of the muscle fibers, which preserves the meat's inherent tenderness. Lower the oven temperature or use indirect heat on the grill to reduce the risk of overcooking meat.

2. Monitor internal temperatures. Reliably-sourced grassfed beef needn't be cooked to the high "doneness" temperatures recommended by the USDA. Experts at the USDA reflexively direct us to make sure our meat is well-done, fearing exposure to food-borne pathogens. Of particular concern is *E.coli*, a potentially harmful, even deadly, bacteria. But empirical evidence suggests this hazard is greatly reduced in grassfed beef. Not only is *E.coli* found in much lower numbers in grassfed meat, it is also a strain that is easily vulnerable to our bodies' natural defenses. Even when *E.coli* is found on grassfed beef, it rarely survives our own digestive acids. Further, grassfed animals are highly unlikely to carry the particularly virulent *E.coli* 0157:H7, because that strain of bacteria evolved in the unnaturally hyper-acidic stomachs of grain-fed factory-farmed beef.

How rare you eat your meat is a personal choice. As much as I might like to, I cannot dictate how you run your kitchen. That said, I advocate for internal cooked meat temperatures that are significantly lower than the USDA guidelines for "doneness." The chart below contains two different internal temperature ranges: one lists USDA recommendations, and the other shows my own preferences. The results are tastier and easier to digest. If the internal temperatures I suggest are too low for your comfort, feel free to use the USDA guidelines, unless I'm coming to dinner!

MEAT	Suggested Internal Temperatures for Grassfed and Pastured Meats	USDA Recommended Internal Temperatures
Beef, Bison	120–140° F	145–170°F
Ground Meat	160° F	160°F
Veal	125–155°F	145–170°F
Lamb and Goat	120–145°F	145–170°F
Pork	145–160°F	145–170°F
Chicken (unstuffed)	165°F	165°F
Turkey (unstuffed)	165°F	165°F

3. Understand which cuts require which cooking methods. The appropriate cooking method depends on where a cut of meat comes from on the animal. If it comes from a muscle that works hard, such as the shoulder, the neck or the shanks, it will contain more connective tissue, which can make meat tough. Connective tissue typically requires cooking in liquid to break down. Thus, the cuts of hardworking muscle require moist-heat cooking methods, such as braising, barbecuing (which is different from grilling), smoking, slow-cooking ("Crock-Potting") or stewing. The exception to this is Super Slow Roasting, a cooking method I'll discuss later, in which a normally tough cut of meat is tenderized by low temperature oven cooking that "braises" the meat in its own contained juices.

By contrast, the muscles that do the least amount of work, such as the tenderloin and most steaks and chops, are the most tender meats. These cuts actually need exposure to enough heat to *firm* the muscle fibers for you to enjoy them. Thus, steaks, chops and most roasts from the loin or legs of grassfed and pastured animals require dry-heat methods, such as grilling, pan-frying or roasting. . . . Just make sure the flame isn't too intense!

Finally, I'd like to suggest minimizing the use of intense seasonings and heavy sauces. As a cookbook author, I always feel a bit strange offering this advice when my charge is to generate a few hundred different recipes for cooking meat. The obvious way to do that is through variations of seasonings. However, if you'll browse through the coming chapters, you'll notice that the basic cuts—the steaks and the roasts—are nearly always presented first with the sparest seasonings: salt, pepper, perhaps some garlic and herbs. Minimizing seasoning will highlight those inherent flavors of grassfed meats described earlier, which are truly delightful. If you are new to grassfed meat, I encourage you to start with simpler recipes so that you can experience that taste. Then, as you progress to the more sophisticated recipes, your palate will be able to detect the flavor of the good meat you are working with as you pair seasonings that enhance, rather than obscure it.

Learning to work with every cut of beef can be daunting. The variety of cuts seems endless, and the names of the cuts vary from region to region. Sadly, customers' insecurities about working with everything on the beef animal results in a lot of meat going unsold. Farmers may find that they quickly run out of rib eye and Porterhouse steaks, but are left with a surplus of London broils and chuck roasts. In my experience, although these cuts are equally delicious, the customers are simply unsure of how to prepare them.

There is an easy way to get over this insecurity: learn which muscles do what work. Get down on all fours on your living room floor, or if you want to feel more authentic and the weather is nice, head out to your yard or a nearby park. Crawl around and pretend to eat the grass. As you do so, pay attention to which muscles move the most, and which muscles move the least. Those muscles that move the most—the

cuts from the **chuck** (as you crawl around, that would be your shoulders), the **foreleg** and **brisket** (those would be your arms and chest), and the **plate** and **flank** (your belly area)—are all doing the most work. They are propelling your body forward, lifting your neck up and down, enabling you to be a happy, active, grazing cow (or steer, as the case may be). All of these cuts are commonly regarded as the "tougher cuts," which is a very unfair designation. If they are slapped across the grate of a flaming hot grill, they may be tough. But, if they are slow-cooked in a little wine or broth, they become some of the most tender meat you will ever eat. This is because these cuts, to do their job of helping the beef move about, contain connective tissue, commonly called "grizzle," interwoven among the muscles. Connective tissue requires moist heat to break down. Thus, these cuts are ideal for slow cooking, pot roasting, braising, or stewing. They will also be suitable candidates for **super-slow roasting**, as explained in Chapter Four. If intense beef flavor is your goal, these are the ideal selections. Cuts from these primal areas include **stew beef, brisket, short ribs, chuck roasts, arm pots, ground beef,** and **shanks.** They also include **skirt** and **flank** steaks, which are very thin steaks that are often marinated and cooked rare using a dry heat method, and are prized for their robust flavor and chewy texture.

Okay, stay down on the ground. Don't get up yet. Graze a little more. As you do, pay attention to what other muscles are working. While the shoulders and forelegs do most of the work, the hind legs and rump must move along with them. Muscles from the **round** (that would be your rump and the top of your thighs) are active, but they don't do the bulk of the beef's grazing work. They just follow from behind. They are not the most tender parts of the beef, nor are they the chewiest. These cuts can be roasted using conventional methods, but I find them perfect for **super-slow roasting**. They can also be marinated and grilled, or sliced super-thin into **sandwich steaks** (also called **minute steaks** or **skillet steaks**—thin slices of beef that can be fried in under a minute). Cuts from this primal area include **top-, bottom-** and **eye-round roasts**; **sandwich steaks, stew beef, ground beef,** and **London broils**. While it is technically not part of the same primal, I include the **sirloin tip** in this area as well. The sirloin tip is located right next to the round. It is not as tender as the actual sirloin primal, and is cooked using the same methods as for the round. Sirloin tips can be done in roasts or steaks, or as **kebabs**, perfect for marinating and grilling.

Are you still grazing out on your lawn? Good. Now let's focus on what muscles *aren't* moving much as you browse the pasture. The middle part of your body, all along your back, doesn't have to do much work. On the beef, the primal just behind the shoulders would be the rib primal (where **rib eye steaks** and **rib roasts** originate), followed by the **short loin** (home of the most tender cuts—**filet mignon steaks, tenderloin roasts, top loin** or **NY strip, Porterhouse,** and **T-bone steaks**). Behind the short loin is the **sirloin**, the primal where **sirloin steaks** and **roasts** are cut. All the cuts from these primals are the most tender parts of the animal. Cuts from the short loin will be the most tender with the least amount of flavor, and cuts from the rib eye and sirloin will be slightly less tender, but with more marbling and flavor. All of them are suited well to dry-heat cooking methods, like pan frying, roasting, or grilling.

Now that you know how the body of a grazing beef works, it should be relatively easy to select a cut at your farmers' market. If the name of the cut is not the same as what I mentioned here (there is tremendous regional variability in the nomenclature), ask the farmer or butcher where it came from on the animal. Once you have that information, picture yourself crawling around again, vision where that muscle would be on the animal, and you'll know whether to select a dry heat, moist heat, or super-slow cooking method.

CHAPTER THREE

Bones and Fat

When most people think of cooking grassfed beef, they first imagine steaks on the grill or roasts in the oven. But before we go there, I'd like you to consider two beef ingredients that are at the foundation of nearly all grassfed cuisine: the bones and the fat. To overlook these treasures is to let about 20% of the entire carcass weight go to waste. To me, that is a tragic loss of the full benefits the animal has given us and, as such, dishonors the sacrifice it has made of its life. Further, it is a disservice to ourselves, since bones and fat offer vital nutrients, help to stretch our meat budget considerably, and they'll make grassfed cuisine taste even more delicious!

Good bone broth forms the basis of many of the recipes you will see in this book. I strongly urge you to buy bones from your farmer and to save every leftover bone from anything you cook, and use them to make your own broth. As you will see, it is very easy to do. Real bone broth draws minerals from bone, cartilage, marrow and any added vegetables, and converts them to electrolytes, ionic solutions that are easily absorbed into the body. Broth also contains proteinaceous gelatin that supplies hydrophilic colloids, which attract your stomach's digestive juices to the surface of cooked food particles (this is especially helpful for folks suffering from intestinal disorders). Better still, the gelatin in bone broth helps the body fully assimilate any other proteins that are ingested, drawing more nutrition from each bite of meat. By helping your body to go farther on less meat, you also stretch your food dollars. Further, broth is also a great remedy for the symptoms of colds, flu, gastroenteritis and even joint pain and bone injuries.

Beef suet is rich in fat soluble vitamins A, D, E, and K, which help us to absorb minerals from our food. When suet is rendered into tallow, it is the single best fat for greasing your skillet prior to searing a steak or burger, because it can reach a high temperature before it starts smoking in the pan. It tastes delicious in holiday plum and Yorkshire puddings, it can be crumbled into biscuit dough or melted into cornbread batter, and further still, it makes excellent salve and soap, and even candles.

THE ELEMENTS OF BROTH

The Italians have an expression, "Tutto fa brodo"—"Everything is broth." Nearly anything you can find in your kitchen can be added to a broth to enrich its flavor and nutritional value. The five basic elements are bones, vegetables, herbs, acid and water.

Bones. Naturally, this is the most essential ingredient. Many mistakenly believe that only the marrow bones make good stock. While marrow does add lots of flavor and minerals, a variety of different bones is ideal. "Knuckle" bones (leg joints) and oxtails are a great source of gelatin; neck, rib and other meaty bones add color and flavor, as does that leftover bone from Friday night's rib eye steak, or the remains from Sunday's leg of lamb. For an extra calcium boost, I often save egg shells and add them to the pot, as well. Once all the meat, bones, shells and vegetables have simmered in the pot for several hours, they'll be strained from the complete broth and discarded; virtually all of their nutritive value is in the liquid.

Be creative with your broth. A pure beef or chicken stock is lovely, but some of the most exciting dishes result from mixing varieties of bones, using anything that is on hand—a few lamb bones, perhaps a chicken carcass, mixed in with some pork chop leftovers . . . all create a dynamic broth flavor. Long ago in France, cooks had la bouilloire éternelle—the "eternal kettle," a large broth pot that never left the fire. If a piece of chicken was taken out, then new chicken was added; the same with a piece of beef or a slab of pork. Whenever broth was removed from the kettle, water was added, yielding a steady supply of delicious stock and a ready liquid medium for cooking meats with moist-heat methods. Incorporating all different kinds of meats when making stock eases your work (you don't need to sort your leftover bones according to animal type), reduces waste and creates complex flavor. Most of the recipes in this book call for "meat broth." I've discovered that all the different mixes of bones will taste equally delicious, so there is no need to make extra labor for yourself.

Vegetables. Leftover cooked vegetables can go into the pot, along with fresh veggies, and even those errant odds and ends that might be on the cusp of spoiling. Open your produce drawer and be generous to your stock—broccoli about to flower, carrots gone floppy; peppers, tomatoes and onions growing soft on the kitchen counter. Set aside carrot tops and tips for the broth, as well as the woody ends of broccoli stalks, or the outer leaves of cabbage that may be a bit marred from the garden. Don't be fussy, as they will all be discarded (hopefully composted) once their flavors and minerals have been captured by the broth.

Herbs. Herbs, whether fresh or dried, add both flavor and nutrients to your broth. One tablespoon of fresh herbs is equivalent to one teaspoon dried herb. However, if you don't have any on hand, don't let that stop you from making broth!

Acid and Water. Once the vegetables, herbs and bones have been added to the stock pot, fill it with water, then pour in an acid, such as vinegar or wine. Use as little as a tablespoon of vinegar, or as much as a few cups of wine, depending on your taste. Allow the stock to stand for 30 minutes to an hour *before* cooking, so the acid can draw minerals out of the bones and into the broth; this also enhances the flavor.

Bring the stock to a simmer, keeping it covered. The longer you can simmer your stock, the better: twelve hours will be sufficient, but seventy-two hours will be even better. If the pot gets too low on liquid, add more water. Once it is complete, you have a wonderful base for cooking soups, for cooking rice, grains and legumes, for a hot beverage, or for braising those other luscious (and inexpensive) bone-in cuts of meat so often overlooked: shanks, necks, oxtails, bone-in shoulders, or ribs. To magnify the intensity of its flavors and to save storage space, you can take the broth to the next level by reducing it down to a demi-glace (see below).

Meat Broth

MAKES 5 QUARTS

4–6 pounds bones (Beef, lamb, pork or poultry bones will all work. Ideally, some will be raw and some will be precooked from previous meals, which will add a rich color and flavor dimension.)

2 large carrots, scrubbed and unpeeled, cut into large chunks

3 ribs celery, cut into large chunks, leafy tops included

2 medium onions, halved (if onions are clean, feel free to leave the skins on)

8 quarts water

3–4 sprigs fresh thyme

3–4 sprigs oregano

3 cloves garlic, crushed but not peeled (optional)

1 medium tomato, coarsely chopped (optional)

Any other leftover vegetables you might have lying around (except maybe for lettuce)

2 teaspoons coarse salt

3 tablespoons red wine vinegar or cider vinegar (or 1–2 cups wine)

Here is a classic broth recipe that diligently makes use of the standard repertoire of ingredients. Remember: the list of ingredients in this case is really only a suggestion. Improvise with what you have on hand!

Add all the above ingredients to a very large stockpot. Allow all the ingredients to rest for 30 minutes to one hour before turning the flame under the pot to medium. This step will enable the acids in the vinegar or wine to draw the minerals from the bones.

Bring the mixture to a boil slowly, skimming off any froth that rises to the surface. Reduce the heat to low, and slowly simmer the broth for a minimum of 12 hours. The longer you cook it, the richer it will be. If your cooktop will allow a slow, steady simmer and you will be nearby, consider allowing the mixture to slowly bubble, with the lid in place, for about three days straight, adding water as necessary.

If you don't feel secure leaving the pot untended overnight, simmer the stock all day, or while you are home. Turn it off before going to bed or leaving, then resume simmering it when you are around once more. Be vigilant about adding additional water if the fluid level gets too low. (Personally, if the cooking is interrupted for less than 12 hours, I leave the stock unrefrigerated on the stove, as I know it will be returned to a high enough temperature to kill food-borne pathogens. If this practice makes you uncomfortable, simply refrigerate your stock between simmer sessions.)

When the final simmering is complete, pour the broth through a sieve to strain out all the bones, vegetables and herbs.

Pour the broth into jars, or return it to the stove top and simmer once more, uncovered, until the volume is reduced to about 5 quarts for a more concentrated broth. Chill for several hours. Ideally, once it is cold it should be mildly gelatinous. A layer of fat will have solidified on the surface.

Remove the fat layer prior to using. If you like, it can be saved and used to sauté vegetables and meat. Once you have skimmed the fat off your broth, store it in the refrigerator or freezer.

Shannon's Meat Broth

6–8 pounds pre-roasted bones

1 large onion

1 large carrot

4 cups mixed greens

½ cup cider vinegar

8 quarts water

The above broth recipe is perfect if you are the type of person who likes to do things right. I'm the type of person who likes to do things simply. In my family, we drink about one gallon of broth per week, plus what we use for soups, stews, braises and sauces. That means I'm making broth year-round, a couple of times per week, and I don't always have all the necessary ingredients on hand. In the interest of working with what's usually in my fridge, here's a shortened version.

I prepare it using the same instructions as *Basic Meat Broth.*

A NOTE TO THE FRUGAL: To help my vegetable dollars go farther, I don't use first-quality produce in my broth. I save the onion skins and ends from other dishes I've cooked, as well as the carrot tops and tips, and the woody stems and ribs of the greens. I collect them in a bag all week, and by the time I'm ready to start a new batch of broth, there's usually plenty of vegetable scraps to make this recipe.

DEMI-GLACE, SHANNON-STYLE

If asked to select the single most important ingredient in my kitchen, if without broth, it would have to be the little glass tub of demi-glace that jiggles in the back corner of my refrigerator. Admittedly, I use the term casually—a French chef would likely have me strung up by my toes for awarding this wondrous gelatinous blob such a name. By definition, a true demi-glace is a brown sauce made by first concocting an espagnole sauce, then blending it with an estouffade, or clear soup, then making a reduction. My version of a demi-glace (if you will allow me the privilege of the term) is simply done by making a vat of broth, straining out the bones, etc., then bringing it to a rolling boil until it has reduced to just a few cups, monitoring often to make sure it doesn't scorch.

Ordinarily, when I chill broth, I skim off the fat that settles on the top; I do *not* do this with demi-glace. Since it will be kept for a long time in the refrigerator, I allow the fat to solidify over the surface, which seals it for longer storage in the manner of a *confit*. If I discover a little mold growing on this surface layer of fat, I spoon it off, add it to the compost, then bravely move forward with dinner preparations. I don't let gastronomic rules, pretensions and regulations interfere with my quest for a good repast.

While a jury of French chefs may convict me of gastronomic heresy, I have every faith that an army of French housewives would scurry to my defense, brandishing their stockpots and wooden spoons with intimidating valor. Most French chefs aren't trying to get a preschooler to stop playing with the kitchen knives, another daughter to learn her addition and subtraction, fixing lunch, scheduling appointment dates on the telephone, and turning out a serviceable demi-glace all at the same time. I daresay that, if faced with those daily challenges, most French chefs would probably choose the Shannon Hayes "semi-demi-glace" technique as well.

Demi-glace, made in my inelegant way, is an amazing ingredient. It concentrates all the benefits of a rich, nourishing broth down to a small, easily stored and preserved volume that can then be reconstituted to add flavor and nutrients to nearly all my dishes. When the kids are swapping winter flu germs, I add 3–6 tablespoons of my demi-glace to 2–3 cups of water to make them a lovely clear stock to sip (taste and add more demi-glace or water until the strength is to your liking). I toss a few tablespoons into the water when preparing beans, rice and legumes. I use it to make gravies and pan sauces even richer. Reconstituted in water, the demi-glace performs just like meat broth, and spares a lot of space in your refrigerator and freezer.

Roasted Marrow Bone Gremolata

SERVES 8

6–10 pieces of beef or veal marrowbones, about 1 pound

1 cup minced fresh parsley

1 cup finely crushed walnuts

2 cloves minced garlic

2 tablespoons lemon zest

Coarse salt, to taste

Carrot sticks, endive leaves or toast points, for serving, optional

Marrowbones have long been regarded as a rich indulgence by epicureans-in-the-know. While they were spurned in recent years for their high fat content, grassfed enthusiasts eager to find sources of those healthful grassfed fats are rediscovering them. According to Ramiel Nagel, author of Cure Tooth Decay, *bone marrow from grassfed animals can also be very helpful in re-mineralizing teeth, reversing tooth decay. Nagel explains the marrow contains stem cells that help to rejuvenate the body and promote bone growth. Whether true or not, roasted bone marrow is delicious, especially when served as part of this fresh parsley and walnut gremolata.*

Preheat the oven to 375° F. Set the marrow bones in a cast-iron skillet and roast 20–25 minutes, until the marrow starts to bubble. Some bones might take longer to roast than others, depending on their size. If necessary, remove the smaller bones earlier. Otherwise, the fat will render out and the remaining marrow will get chewy.

Remove the bones from the oven. Allow them to cool while you combine the parsley, walnuts, garlic and lemon zest. Using a butter knife or a small spoon, scrape out the bone marrow and add it to the gremolata. Mix well. Season to taste with the coarse salt. Serve as a dip with carrot sticks, spooned onto endive leaves, or spread on crackers or on toast points.

NOTE: Save these bones, as well as any bones from roasts and steaks, and add them to your next batch of broth. We keep a large plastic bag in the freezer for collecting whatever bone treasures remain after meals.

Holiday Pudding with Rum Sauce

ADVANCE PREPARATION REQUIRED

SERVES 16

½ cup golden raisins

½ pound dried apricots or prunes, cut into pieces

½ pound dried cranberries

½ pound pitted dates, cut into pieces

¾ cup grated raw carrots

Grated zest of ½ orange

Grated zest of ½ lemon

½ cup sherry

2 cups finely chopped pecans or walnuts

8 ounces minced tallow

3 eggs

¼ cup milk or heavy cream

1 teaspoon cinnamon

⅛ teaspoon allspice

1 teaspoon fine salt

1 cup cooked mashed potatoes or sweet potatoes

Rum Sauce (recipe follows)

This is one of our Christmas favorites, a twist on the traditional Christmas pudding. It has been adapted to our family's dietary needs: there is no flour or added sugar, but the fat—tallow in this case—happily, has stayed put.

Preheat the oven to 350° F. Combine the fruits, carrot, and orange and lemon zests in a large bowl. Add the sherry and let stand for at least 1 hour. Meanwhile, mix the nuts and tallow together, then mix them into the sherry-soaked fruit. Beat the eggs, milk, cinnamon, allspice and salt together, then gradually blend them into the mashed potatoes. Using your hands or a wooden spoon, thoroughly combine the potatoes with the fruit.

Divide the mixture into 2 well-greased 1-quart pudding molds (coffee cans or stainless steel bowls will suffice). Fill them ¾ full. Cover tightly with aluminum foil. Place the pudding molds on a rack in a large pot. Add enough boiling water to the pot to come halfway up sides of mold. Cover the pot and steam pudding over medium-low heat until tester inserted into center comes out clean, about 2 hours, adding more boiling water to pot if necessary.

Remove foil, transfer mold to rack, and cool 5 minutes. Turn out the puddings onto ovenproof platters or baking pans. Cool completely, then cover and refrigerate, allowing the flavors to ripen, for 2 days, or up to one week. Before serving, reheat in a 200-degree oven for about 45 minutes, or until heated through. Serve with Rum Sauce. Unused portions can be stored up to 6 months in the freezer.

Rum Sauce

1 cup heavy cream

3 egg yolks

2 tablespoons honey

½ teaspoon fine salt

⅓ cup rum

Prepare the bottom half of a double boiler with 1 inch of water and bring it to a simmer. Add all the ingredients to the top part of a double boiler and whisk well. Put the top boiler over the bottom half and whisk continuously until the sauce thickens. Serve immediately.

HOW TO RENDER FAT

As I mentioned earlier, beef suet, rendered into tallow, is useful for more than the occasional holiday pudding. It is great for pan frying and baking, and is the primary ingredient for the soap and salve recipes which follow. Thus, before we move on, let's learn the simple method to properly render it so that it will be more useful.

Once you've acquired a nice big bag of fat (I like to work in volumes of 5–9 pound batches), settle into your kitchen and cut it into small pieces, ideally less than one inch long, taking care to discard any fleshy or fibrous spots. Toss the good bits into your pot until it is no more than ⅔ full. It has been said that heavy pots (such as cast iron) are best for rendering, but I've come to favor a lighter, good-quality stainless-steel pot. It is easier and safer to carry, and cleanup is a breeze.

Many books instruct you to layer your fat on top of water to prevent it from burning, but I've found this step unnecessary. Most modern stoves have a simmer burner that will cook the fat at a low enough temperature to prevent scorching. If your stove doesn't have this, then use a slow-cooker. To help ensure a bright ivory white color, sprinkle a half-teaspoon of baking soda over the fat. Turn the heat on to the lowest possible setting and put the lid on the pot, leaving it slightly ajar so that steam escapes. Simmer for several hours, returning every 90 minutes or so to stir it carefully with a wooden spoon. After about 4 hours (more or less, depending on the amount you're preparing), you will notice that the cracklings—browned bits of crisped fat—will float to the surface. This is your cue to turn off the heat. Allow the fat to partially cool while you set a colander over a large stainless-steel, porcelain, or glass bowl (not plastic). Line the colander with cheese cloth, then pour the fat through, straining out all the cracklings and leaving a clear, golden liquid in the bowl. Let the fat cool 5–10 minutes longer before pouring it into wide-mouthed containers to be stored in the refrigerator or freezer. To keep your fat from souring, store it in a cool, dark place. Rendered fat will keep up to *two years* in a refrigerator, or indefinitely in the freezer.

Honey–Oatmeal Farmers' Soap

11.5 ounces lye

32 ounces cold water

5 pounds rendered beef fat (tallow), or tallow mixed with a combination of lard and/or rendered lamb fat

2 ounces essential oil of your choice (for scent)

½ cup ground oats

½ cup raw honey, slightly warmed

EQUIPMENT:

1 40-ounce heat-resistant glass jar (a clean glass juice jar is perfect)

Safety glasses

1 old wooden spoon

2 thermometers

1 large shoebox

1 garbage bag

1 bench knife

Kitchen scale

No, you can't eat it, but this basic thrifty recipe for tallow soap helped Bob and me pay off our mortgage while maintaining terrific complexions. We saved money by not having to buy soap, and we sold the surplus to our customers. Soaps made from super-saturated beef fat last a long time and are great for the skin. If you don't have enough beef fat for a full batch, you can mix in lard or rendered lamb fat.

Two hours before you plan to make the soap, select a well-ventilated work surface where you won't be troubled if there is a potential lye spill (perhaps an old cutting board or outdoor picnic table). Ideally, choose a location and work time when children and pets will not be around to distract you or potentially get burned from the lye.

An hour or two before you make the soap, set the jar on a scale and pour in the lye granules until you have 11.5 ounces. Wearing your safety glasses, slowly add the cold water, taking care to protect your eyes and not breathe in the fumes. Stir rapidly with the handle of an old wooden spoon (it will become scarred and burned, so don't use your best spoon), until the lye is completely in solution. Set it aside and allow it to cool. Keep the solution and any leftover lye granules far away from children. Using rubber gloves to prevent burning your hands, wash the spoon thoroughly.

Meanwhile, melt the tallow in a large stainless steel pot over a low flame until it is about 80 percent liquefied. Turn off the flame and allow the remaining fat to melt in the ambient heat. Once the fat is liquefied, begin monitoring the temperature as it cools. When it is around 110 degrees, set the glass jar of lye in a basin of hot water.

Monitor the temperature of the melted fat as it falls, and the lye solution as it rises. Once both are between 112 and 115 degrees, you are ready to use the lye to saponify the fat.

Using your wooden spoon (right-side-up this time), begin stirring the fat in a steady circular motion, adding the lye in a slow stream. Continue the circular stirring after all the lye is added to make sure the lye contacts all the fat in the pot. The mixture will turn opaque. Once the fat is opaque, continue stirring constantly for about 30 minutes, until the mixture thickens to the consistency of pea soup and it "traces," or leaves a trail across the surface, when you lift the spoon out of the pot. Stir in the essential oil, oats and honey.

Line the shoebox with the garbage bag. The bag should come up and over the sides.

Pour the soap into your new "soap mold" and fold the plastic bag gently over the top of the liquid. Cover your soap mold with a piece of cardboard or Styrofoam, then with some blankets and towels. The idea is to insulate the mold so that the heat escapes very slowly.

After 24 hours, remove the blankets, turn the soap out on a cutting board, and use a bench knife to cut it into bars. Leave the bars someplace where the air can circulate around them freely for a minimum of two weeks (longer is even better). Use a sharp paring knife to shave off the powdery layer of soda ash that may settle on the outside of the bars before you take it into the bath.

World's Best Bay Rum Shaving Soap

6¾ ounces lye

17 ounces water

4 ounces castor oil

4 ounces tallow

4 ounces coconut oil

27 ounces lard

12 ounces olive oil

1 ounce bay essential oil

¼ ounce lime essential oil

3 tablespoons bentonite clay

EQUIPMENT:

1 40-ounce heat-resistant glass jar (a clean glass juice jar is perfect)

Safety glasses

1 old wooden spoon

2 thermometers

Soap molds (enough for 18 (3-ounce) bars)

Several pieces of cardboard cut large enough to cover each soap mold

Kitchen scale

My dad grows a thick beard and has long struggled to find a good shaving soap or cream that allows for a clean shave without irritating his skin. As it turns out, he didn't need to look any farther than the barnyard. This shaving soap makes use of rendered tallow and lard, making it cheap to produce, but far superior to any product available conventionally. And it lasts a very long time, too! It takes my dad about one year of daily shaves to go through a single 3-ounce bar. This recipe will yield 18 (3-ounce) bars. Milky Way Molds out of Portland, Oregon, sells beautiful 3-ounce round soap molds that fit perfectly into any shaving cup. This recipe calls for bentonite clay, which helps give the soap the extra slip it needs to get over bristly whiskers. Bentonite clay can be found at most health food stores, or online from Frontier Natural Products Co-op.

To prep the lye, select a work surface where you won't be troubled if there is a potential lye spill (perhaps an old cutting board or outdoor picnic table). Ideally, choose a location and work time when children and pets will not be around to distract you or potentially get burned from the lye.

An hour or two before you make the soap, set the jar on the kitchen scale and pour in the lye granules until you have 6¾ ounces. Wearing your safety glasses, slowly add the water, taking care to protect your eyes and not breathe in the fumes. Stir rapidly with the handle of an old wooden spoon (it will become scarred and burned, so don't use your best spoon), until the lye is completely in solution. Set it aside and allow it to cool.

Keep the solution and any leftover lye granules far away from children. Using rubber gloves to prevent burning your hands, wash the spoon thoroughly.

Meanwhile, melt the fat and oils in a large stainless-steel pot over a low flame until it is about 80 percent liquefied. Turn off the flame and allow the remaining fat to melt in the ambient heat. Once the fat is liquefied, begin monitoring the temperature as it cools. When the fat is around 105 degrees, set the glass jar of lye in a basin of hot water.

Monitor the temperature of the melted fat as it falls, and the lye solution as it rises. Once both are between 96 and 100 degrees, you are ready to use the lye to saponify the fat.

Using your wooden spoon (right-side-up this time), begin stirring the fat in a steady circular motion, adding the lye in a slow stream.★ Continue the circular stirring after all the lye is added to make sure the lye contacts all the fat in the pot. The mixture will turn opaque. Once the fat is opaque, continue stirring constantly for about 30–60 minutes until the mixture thickens to the consistency of thick pea soup and it "traces," or leaves a trail across the surface, when you lift the spoon out of the pot. Stir in the essential oils and bentonite clay.

Spoon the soap batter into the molds. Once you have filled an entire mold tray, cover it with a sheet of cardboard, set the next mold on top, and continue filling. In the end you will have a tower of about 6 filled trays sandwiched with layers of cardboard. Wrap the tray tower in a blanket. The idea is to insulate the soaps so that the heat escapes very slowly.

After 24 hours, remove the blanket and turn the soap out of the molds. Leave the bars someplace where the air can circulate around them freely for a minimum of two weeks before using.

★ To enable slow pouring, we use a glass juice jar with a lid, into which we have made two ¼-inch holes at opposite points: one for pouring a thin stream and one for air to enter the jar.

Tallow Salve

1 tablespoon dried comfrey leaf

1 tablespoon dried comfrey root

1 tablespoon dried lavender blossoms

1½ tablespoons dried nettle leaves

8 ounces tallow

8 ounces olive oil

2–3 disposable tea filters (1-cup size)

It so happened that one night, after spending the day rendering beef tallow for soap, I was reading the book Calico Bush with my daughters at bedtime. In this old story, the main characters had just been in a storm at sea and had been badly beaten and bruised. As a remedy, they rubbed tallow on their aches and bruises. My mind immediately went to those pots of freshly rendered fat in my fridge . . . could there be another use for it? After the kids were tucked in, I snuck downstairs to do some research on the computer and discovered that tallow salves were common in the old west, as well as in Europe. The next day, I blended a batch and left some at the farm for my parents. My mother had been planting garlic bulbs all morning, and by evening, her hands were aching and sore. She rubbed the salve into her skin and within the hour her pain began to abate. We now use this as a salve for chapped and dry skin, as well as a go-to remedy for scrapes, aches and bruises.

If you don't have these herbs in your backyard or home medicine chest, they are usually available in the bulk section of most health food stores, or online through Frontier Natural Products Co-op. This recipe makes 16 ounces of salve.

Place the herbs in the tea filters and add them to a slow cooker, along with the tallow and olive oil. Cook on the lowest setting for six hours. Remove the herbs and tea filters and add them to your compost. Pour the salve into wide-mouthed jars.

Be sure not to dump any excess drippings down your drain, as the hardening fat can accumulate over time and eventually generate a plumbing nightmare. Instead, wipe the crock out thoroughly with a paper towel. Discard the towel in your compost, and wash out your crock normally.

TALLOW CANDLES

Growing up in one of the former original thirteen colonies, I often heard stories about how the early Americans made their way in the new world. Tallow candles were a common source of light among those who could not afford beeswax or bayberry. On school field trips, we'd visit living history museums where some of these candles would be on display. Their creamy surface called out to my fingers. I longed to touch them. I wanted to see them lit. "Don't bother," costumed museum guides would tell me, "tallow candles melt too easily, they break easily, they're smoky, and they stink."

Each time I rendered a pot of tallow, I remembered those candles and longed to challenge the modern conventional wisdom. In 2011, while exploring new value-added enterprises for our farm, I decided to give it a try. But rather than using pure tallow, I blended it with beeswax. The first attempt, made with two parts tallow and one part beeswax, left me with droopy candles that broke at the slightest touch. With further experimenting, I discovered that by using equal parts beeswax and tallow, I could make fantastic candles. They were hard, durable, long-lasting, smokeless, and odorless (unless I chose to add a scent). I had the finest properties of both fats—durability and sweet scent from beeswax, and thrifty ingredients from the tallow. Best of all, the candles had the beautiful creamy finish of the old-fashioned tallow candles, making them a sensuous pleasure for the eyes as well as the hands.

This 50:50 tallow-beeswax blend works beautifully for homemade hand-dipped candles (if you will be using molds, I recommend using two parts beeswax to 1 part tallow). I recommend getting a copy of the Storey Country Wisdom Bulletin, *Making Hand-Dipped Candles* by Betty Oppenheimer for simple easy-to-follow instructions to get started. Instead of using her beeswax/paraffin/stearic acid formulas, use the simple 50% beeswax:50% tallow formula I've outlined here, and follow the rest of her instructions. You'll love the results.

CHAPTER FOUR
Pan-Frying and Oven-Roasting

When customers transition from factory-farmed meat to grassfed, they seem to first run into trouble with the dry-heat techniques methods, including pan-frying and oven-roasting. It is not that the grassfed beef has something inherently wrong with it. To the contrary, it has something right with it, and we just need to learn how to use that to our advantage in the kitchen.

Let's examine first what's wrong with factory-farmed beef, and how you have learned to compensate for it in your kitchen. Factory-farmed beef is finished in confinement settings, where the animals move very little, which causes their muscles to atrophy. That doesn't mean your steaks and roasts will be more tender, as many factory-farm boosters claim. It means the meat will be more mushy—and flavorless. Americans have simply gotten used to this. We don't expect to chew very much, and we tend to rely on heavy seasonings to give our dishes the flavor they are lacking. Furthermore, because the livestock are on a steady grain diet, the acidity of their stomach is unnaturally high. The *Escherichia coli* bacteria that can survive in the stomach of a grainfed beef is therefore an acid-resistant strain, very often the virulent form, famously known as *E. coli* 0157:H7. To protect Americans from getting sick when they eat factory-farmed beef, the USDA has instructed us to cook our factory-farmed meat to the point of becoming a flavorless, dry, hunk of gray char. Therefore, as a result of muscle atrophy and *E. coli*, Americans have expectations in the kitchen that their meat will be cooked until it is gray, and that the "mushiness" they detect when chewing is actually tenderness, and they've been conditioned to season it like crazy to make up for a lack of flavor. Yuck.

By contrast, let's look at what is *right* with grassfed steaks and roasts, and how that plays out in your kitchen. When you choose a grassfed steak or roast, one of the first things to notice is the integrity of the muscle fibers. When you slice a piece of properly cooked steak from an animal that has gotten daily exercise roaming in pastures, the muscle fibers will stand more erect. The meat will be tender, but there will be muscle integrity and species-specific flavor. Over time, your palate will come to discern the difference between a truly tender piece of meat, and a mushy one. The other important factor is that because grassfed animals do not receive any grain in their diet, the virulent acid-resistant strain of *E. coli* 0157:H7 is highly unlikely to develop in their stomachs. That means you need not cook your meat until it is gray. Hence, you derive the nutrition and flavor benefits of not overcooking your meat. It is particularly important not to overcook grassfed, as those healthy muscle fibers will contract with over-exposure to heat. Once meat crosses an internal doneness temperature of 145 degrees Fahrenheit, the muscle fibers contract at an accelerated rate, drying out your steaks and roasts even faster. Thus, as you'll see in these recipes, I encourage you to keep your steaks rare to medium-rare. If you absolutely insist that you can't enjoy meat unless it is well-done, use an instant-read meat thermometer and cook it to 145 degrees, taking care not to exceed that figure (or you will dry it out).

The best benefit of eating meat raised in harmony with nature is its flavor. The intensity of the minerals, the sweet herby flavor from the grasses and the beefy-richness that comes from a healthy, active animal all come through in the meat. That means you don't have to smother your steaks and roasts with overbearing sauces. Very often, all you need is some salt and pepper. As you'll see in the coming recipes, I'm not opposed to sauces and seasonings, but I've taken care to make sure they are not overbearing nor cloyingly sweet. The flavor of your good beef will shine through.

WHAT SIZE ROAST DO I NEED?

If there is one single question that Bob and I need to answer for nearly every customer who visits our farmers' market stall, it is "how much meat do I need?" The simple rule is that if your roast contains a bone, figure on one pound per person; if the roast is boneless, calculate ½ pound per person. Once you've done that basic calculation, consider how many of your dinner companions actually eat meat, whether their appetites are hearty or light, whether there are any small children at the table who won't eat a full helping, and how many extra side dishes will be accompanying the meal. Round up or down based on these factors.

CHOOSING YOUR BEST STEAK

One of our favorite jobs at our farmers' market is helping customers choose the perfect steak to take home for supper. Porterhouse and filet mignon steaks may have the reputation for being "the best," but they are not necessarily the best choice for your dinner needs. The reason they are considered "the best" is because they are tender, and because there are relatively few of them on a beef animal. Other steaks may be a better fit for your taste. If you like lean, tender meat, then **Porterhouse, NY Strips** (aka **Top Loin**), and **filet mignon** may be your best bet. If you like tenderness, but don't mind cutting your meat with a steak knife if it means a little more marbling and flavor, go for the **rib eyes** and **sirloins**. If you are on a budget or need to feed a crowd, **London broils** and **sirloin tip steaks** have very little waste and can go a long way. They are also less expensive, have nice beefy flavor and lend themselves well to marinating. They are best served rare to medium-rare, and should be sliced thinly across the grain when served. **Skirt, hangar** and **flank** steaks are the ideal choices for folks who love robust beefy flavor and are willing to chew a "tougher" piece to taste it. Unfortunately, there are only two skirts and two flanks per animal. Hangar steak, which is a single thin strip of meat that hangs off the diaphragm, is even more uncommon, as it often disintegrates during the dry-age process, and thus the farmer only occasionally has it in stock. If high-flavor, high-texture meats are your top choice, look toward the chuck for some great alternatives. The **flat-iron** and **chuck eye steaks**, both cut from the shoulder, are great bargain cuts with fantastic marbling and lots of flavor.

The Best Steak, Cooked Indoors

1–2 tablespoons coarse salt

2–3 teaspoons ground black pepper

1–2 cloves garlic, minced

2 tablespoons butter, tallow or rendered lamb fat

1 sirloin, sirloin tip, tri-tip, top round or London broil steak; OR 2 shoulder top blade, shoulder petite tender, rib, porterhouse, t-bone, top loin (NY strip), or tenderloin (filet mignon) steaks, cut 1¼ to 1½-inches thick

Steak doesn't have to be a luxury enjoyed only by those folks with enough backyard space to hold a grill. It can be just as delicious cooked indoors (especially if the outdoor grill is under 4 feet of snow).

Combine the salt, pepper and garlic in a small bowl. Rub the mixture into both sides of the steak, then allow the meat to come to room temperature. Preheat the oven to 200° F., then heat a large cast-iron or other ovenproof skillet over a high flame. Once the skillet is so hot that you can see a little smoke rising off it, add the butter and/or fat and sear the steak for 2 minutes on each side.

Turn off the flame and insert an ovenproof meat thermometer into a boneless side of the steak (do not insert it into the top, as there is not enough depth for the thermometer to take an accurate reading). Leaving the steaks in the skillet, place them in the oven and allow them to finish cooking, about 10–20 minutes, until the internal temperature reads 115–135 degrees. Remove the steaks and allow them to rest 5 minutes before carving and serving. The temperature will rise a few more degrees during this time.

Asian-Style Cold Beef Salad

SERVES 4

1 pound green and yellow summer squash, diced and lightly steamed

1 large sweet red pepper, seeded and julienned

2 carrots, shredded

3 cups snow peas, lightly steamed and coarsely chopped (or diced large)

2–3 cups leftover cooked steak, sliced into thin strips

½ cup lemon juice, or ¼ cup lemon juice and ¼ cup orange juice, if you prefer a sweeter flavor

¼ cup tamari (available at specialty grocers, Asian food stores, and some supermarkets)

3 tablespoons toasted sesame oil

1 tablespoon honey or maple syrup

3 teaspoons grated fresh ginger

¼ teaspoon crushed red pepper

1 cup salted cashews

This is a spicy delight for vegetable fans, a cooling meal for a steamy summer afternoon or evening, where you can use up any leftover steak.

Combine the squash, sweet red pepper, carrots, snow peas, and meat in a large bowl. In a separate bowl, whisk together the lemon juice, tamari, sesame oil, honey, ginger, and crushed red pepper. Pour the dressing over the salad and toss well to coat. Serve immediately, garnished with the cashews.

Spiced Chuck Steak with Caramelized Onions

SERVES 4

1 (2–3-pound) bone-in chuck steak

1 batch Coriander-Cinnamon Spice Rub, (see chapter 8).

2 tablespoons lard, tallow, butter or olive oil

4 medium onions, sliced

The chuck steak, ever affordable, is often overlooked by everyone except we farmers, who build up a back-stock of them in our freezers. That's not necessarily a bad thing, because cooked using this super-slow method, it is tender and flavorful. Top it with the caramelized onions, and it is luscious.

Rub the steak all over with the spice rub. Cover and refrigerate at least two hours or, preferably, overnight. Allow it to come to room temperature before you cook it.

Preheat the oven to 170° F. Place the steak in a roasting pan and cook, uncovered, for 30–35 minutes per pound, or until the meat reaches an internal temperature of 120 to 140 degrees.

Turn the oven off and allow the meat to rest and keep warm there while you prepare the onions (because you are working with a super-slow roasting temperature, you needn't worry about overcooking the steak).

Heat a large skillet over a medium flame, add the fat, and swirl to coat. Let it melt and add the onions. They should sizzle as they hit the pan. If they sputter or splatter, lower the flame. Stir well, coating the onions in the fat. Continue to cook 2–3 minutes longer, until the onions have given up two-thirds of their volume in water. Once they start to brown, lower the heat and allow them to caramelize by cooking slowly for 15–20 minutes longer, stirring often. Lower the heat further if they start to burn.

Remove the bone and gristle from the steak, then slice the meat thinly across the grain. Top with the caramelized onions and serve.

Carpaccio with Mayonnaise Sauce

SERVES 4

1½–2 pounds filet mignon or sirloin steak, frozen for a minimum of 2 weeks, then thawed

Fine salt and fresh ground pepper, to taste

1 recipe Mayonnaise, see below

1 teaspoon Worcestershire sauce

1 teaspoon lemon juice

¼ cup milk

4 teaspoons capers

Over the years as I've cooked filet mignon and sirloin steak, I found myself perpetually feeling that the meat was overdone. I was forever craving rarer and rarer meat. Apparently I'm not the first one to feel this way. The Italians have long enjoyed carpaccio, paper-thin strips of raw filet mignon or sirloin steak drizzled with a mayonnaise sauce. Now that I've discovered it, I finally have a suitably rare way to enjoy my filet and sirloin! Since carpaccio is essentially raw beef, this recipe calls for meat that has been frozen for a minimum of two weeks to ensure any potential pathogens are killed.

Trim any fat or gristle from the beef, then allow it to chill in the refrigerator for an hour. Use a sharp knife to cut it into extremely thin (paper thin) slices. Arrange the slices on the plates. Sprinkle lightly with the salt and pepper.

Mix together the mayonnaise, Worcestershire sauce, and lemon juice in a small bowl, and thin it with the milk to your preferred consistency. Drizzle the dressing over the steak, then garnish each plate with capers. Chill until ready to serve.

Mayonnaise

MAKES 1 CUP

1 egg yolk

1 teaspoon mustard

1 teaspoon fine salt

½ teaspoon ground black pepper

1 teaspoon apple cider vinegar

1 teaspoon lemon juice

1 cup olive oil

For years I never attempted to make my own mayonnaise, as I assumed it required the culinary equivalent of an alchemist master. How wrong I was! Follow these directions exactly, and your mayonnaise will be consistently perfect and unbelievably delicious. You will quickly swear off the jarred alternative from the grocery store, I promise!

Place the egg yolk in a shallow bowl and whisk until it lightens to a lovely lemon yellow. Whisk in the mustard, salt, pepper, vinegar and lemon juice.

And now for the magical part: You must drizzle the oil into the egg mixture *extremely* slowly, whisking it all the while. To be exact on just how slow, set a timer for four minutes. During that 4-minute period, you should whisk in no more than ¼ cup of the oil. After that initial period you can drizzle in the remaining ¾ cup a bit faster (about two or three times that initial rate), whisking steadily the entire time. Use immediately or store covered in the refrigerator for up to two days.

Tamari-Ginger Shaved Steaks

SERVES 6

½ cup tamari

2 tablespoons grated fresh ginger

4 tablespoons toasted sesame oil

1 tablespoon honey or maple syrup

2 tablespoons diced shallot, chives, leeks or green onion

4 cloves garlic, peeled

2 tablespoons Mirin (sweet Japanese cooking wine) or sherry

1 tablespoon crushed red pepper (reduce this amount or eliminate it completely if you are serving spice-averse children)

2 pounds shaved steak (thinly sliced round steak)

2 tablespoons peanut oil

Shaved steaks, also called "sandwich steaks," are extremely thin slices of meat that your butcher cuts from the top, bottom and eye round with a rotary meat slicer. They are often used for Philly cheese steak sandwiches, but here they take a fabulous Asian twist that is one of my kids' favorite dishes. Once marinated, they are very quick to cook up. I serve them with stir-fried vegetables and kimchi, a fermented cabbage pickle popular in East Asia.

Add the tamari, ginger, sesame oil, honey, shallot, garlic, mirin and crushed red pepper to the small bowl of a food processor. Puree. Place the marinade in a glass bowl and add the beef. Turn to coat. Marinate for 1–2 hours or overnight (covered) in the refrigerator.

When you are ready to cook the steaks, remove them from the marinade and blot dry. Heat a skillet over a medium flame. Add just enough oil to lubricate the pan, then add the steaks, laying them flat. Take care to cook only a few at a time so that there is ample space around each piece of meat, otherwise it will not brown. Fry 30 seconds per side, or until browned. Repeat with remaining steak, using additional fat if needed. Serve immediately.

Thai Shaved Steaks

SERVES 4

1 recipe Thai Marinade (see chapter 8)

2 pounds shaved steaks (thinly sliced round steak)

2 tablespoons lard, tallow or butter

Thai Dipping Sauce (recipe follows)

Here's an exciting way to turn an inexpensive cut of meat into a flashy dinner.

Place the marinade in a glass bowl and add the beef. Turn to coat. Marinate for 1–2 hours or overnight (covered) in the refrigerator.

When you are ready to cook the steaks, remove them from the marinade and blot dry. Heat a skillet over a medium flame. Add just enough fat to lubricate the pan, then add the steaks, laying them flat. Take care to cook only a few at a time so that there is ample space around each piece of meat, otherwise it will not brown. Fry 30 seconds per side or until browned. Repeat with remaining steak, using additional fat if needed. Serve with the Thai Dipping Sauce.

Thai Dipping Sauce

MAKES ABOUT ¾ TO 1 CUP

2 tablespoons lime juice

2 tablespoons rice wine vinegar

1 tablespoon Tamari or soy sauce

1 teaspoon crushed red pepper

1 tablespoon honey

1 clove garlic, finely minced

1 teaspoon sesame oil

2 tablespoons fresh cilantro, finely chopped

2 tablespoons fresh mint, finely chopped

Whisk all the ingredients together in a small bowl.

Paprika Lime Skillet Steaks

SERVES 4

1 recipe Paprika-Lime Marinade (see chapter 8)

1 pound shaved steak (thinly sliced round steak)

2 tablespoons lard or butter

These brightly flavored steaks fry up fast once they've been marinated. Paired with a side of coleslaw, they make a terrific quick lunch.

Place the marinade in a glass bowl and add the beef. Turn to coat. Marinate for 1–2 hours or overnight (covered) in the refrigerator.

When you are ready to cook the steaks, remove them from the marinade and blot dry. Heat a skillet over a medium flame. Add just enough fat to lubricate the pan, then add the steaks, laying them flat. Take care to cook only a few at a time so that there is ample space around each piece of meat, otherwise it will not brown. Fry 30 seconds per side or until browned. Repeat with remaining steak, using additional fat if needed. Serve immediately.

THE SUPER-SLOW METHOD

Learning how to properly cook lean meat was one of my biggest challenges when I started writing grassfed cookbooks. Conventional cookbooks recommended roasting lean cuts like London broils and eye rounds in a 350-degree oven, and the results were often gray and chewy. I knew there *must* be a better way to prepare grass-fed meat than the recipes I was finding in most of my current cookbooks. But to find it, I couldn't look forward. I had to look backward, to a time when not all meat was grain-fed. That's when I discovered Adelle Davis's 1947 cookbook, *Let's Cook It Right*. Once I had her volume in hand, I was truly able to learn how to cook meat.

Adelle Davis argued that the tougher cuts from the round and the chuck would be tender and delicious if cooked in a very cool oven, ideally at a temperature no greater than 150–160 degrees. Most modern ovens don't go below 170 degrees, but I went ahead and experimented with her technique, choosing to take the roast out of the oven when the internal meat temperature was 125 degrees, far lower than the USDA recommended internal temperature for "rare" meat (145 degrees). It was fantastic.

What had happened?

The meat wasn't overdone. During the cooking process, myofibrillar proteins begin to harden once meat approaches higher internal temperatures. Furthermore, once meat crosses the internal temperature of 145 degrees, the muscle fibers contract at an accelerated rate, drying the roast out. While the USDA recommends that beef be cooked to a minimum temperature of 145 degrees for food safety concerns, it is important to remember that they assume you are eating beef from factory-farmed animals, processed in large batches in industrial slaughterhouses, wherein there is a much greater chance that your dinner could be harboring food-borne pathogens. Since anyone reading this book is likely using reliably-sourced local beef raised on grass (which greatly reduces the risk of disease transmission), I advocate cooking beef to lower internal temperatures.

The oven temperature was super-low. During this super-slow roasting process, the external surface of the meat dries, but moisture is locked in. The oven temperature is so low that the muscles fibers do not contract, which would force the juice out of the meat and into the pan. Thus, the connective tissue in the meat is broken down by the its own juices, resulting in a wonderfully tender roast.

The best part of this method is that it is the absolutely easiest way to cook a roast that I know of. It will work on a London broil, a sirloin tip, an eye round, top round, bottom round, or any chuck roast. It is no-fail. Here's how to do it:

Super-Slow Roasted Beef

Allow ¼–½ pound meat per serving if you are working with a boneless roast.

Allow ¾ pound of meat per serving if you have a bone-in roast

1 beef roast: bone-in chuck, top round, bottom round, eye round, sirloin tip or London broil are all ideal candidates.

Garlic Spice Rub (see chapter 8), or any of the dry rubs listed in chapter 8 that appeal to you, or sea salt and freshly ground black pepper

When I wrote The Grassfed Gourmet Cookbook, *the super-slow roasting method had people talking. Recipe editors from magazines called to verify the food safety (I reviewed it with a meat scientist before publishing), and farmers called to offer their thanks. It is the one foolproof method for cooking any cut of beef.*

Preheat the oven to 170° F. Rub any of the above-mentioned roasts with the Garlic Spice Rub or any dry-rub seasoning blend of your choice, or just use a little salt and pepper. Place the meat in a cast-iron skillet or roasting pan, and roast, uncovered, for 30–40 minutes per pound (leaner roasts and bone-in roasts will cook closer to 30 minutes per pound; fattier cuts will cook closer to 40 minutes per pound). Use an internal meat thermometer to determine when the meat is done to your liking. The internal temperature should be 120–140 degrees.

Since the juices will not have been disturbed when cooking at such low temperatures, there is no need to rest the meat prior to carving. Slice thin to serve.

Garlic-Rubbed Chuck Eye Roast with Horseradish Cream

SERVES 8

1 batch Garlic Spice Rub (see chapter 8)

1 4-pound boneless chuck eye roast

HORSERADISH CREAM

1 cup sour cream

2–4 teaspoons grated horseradish

The chuck eye is an extraordinary cut of beef. It is a piece of rib eye muscle that extends forward into the chuck primal, giving it great marbling and flavor, with a surprising degree of tenderness for a chuck cut. Since one is often able to buy this piece of the rib eye muscle at chuck roast prices, we call it the "poor man's prime rib."

Rub the Garlic Spice Rub all over the meat. If there is any extra, reserve it for another use. Allow the roast to come to room temperature on the kitchen counter while you preheat the oven to 300° F.

Place the meat in a pan and roast, uncovered, for about 24 minutes per pound or until the internal temperature is between 120 and 140 degrees.

To make the horseradish cream sauce, combine the sour cream with 2 teaspoons grated horseradish. Add additional horseradish until it is seasoned to your liking.

Roast Tenderloin of Beef with Goat Cheese

2 tablespoons coarse salt

1 tablespoon ground black pepper

2 tablespoons tallow (preferred), or lard or butter

1 tenderloin roast

1 batch Garlic-Chive Goat Cheese (see Oven Roasted Burgers with Garlic-Chive Goat Cheese)

The filet is the most tender cut on the animal and, as a whole roast, can make for a very elegant meal, especially when paired with Garlic-Chive Goat Cheese (see Oven-Roasted Burgers with Garlic-Chive Goat Cheese for recipe). To figure serving size, allow for ½ pound of meat per person.

Preheat the oven to 200° F. Blot the roast dry, then sprinkle with salt and pepper. Heat a cast-iron skillet or other ovenproof frying pan over high heat. When you see smoke rising off the pan, grease it with the tallow, then add the tenderloin and sear it over high heat 4 minutes per side (total searing time will be 8 minutes).

Place the pan in the oven and roast for approximately 4 minutes per pound, or until a meat thermometer registers about 115 degrees. While some may prefer their beef more well-done, I feel that the delicate flavors of the tenderloin will be significantly more pronounced if the meat is kept *very* rare. Slice the roast and serve with the goat cheese sprinkled on top.

Prime Rib Roast with Yorkshire Pudding

1 recipe Rosemary Herb Rub (see chapter 8).

1 standing rib roast

Yorkshire Pudding (recipe follows)

Horseradish Cream (see Garlic-Rubbed Chuck-Eye Roast with Horseradish Cream)

Christmas in our family begins in the fall, when my dad and I examine the rib primal of every beef that we process, searching out the perfect standing rib roast. When we make our choice, I write NOT FOR SALE—SHANNY'S MEAT! all across the packaging, and we go into the dark months reassured that our favorite holiday feast is already in the freezer. When estimating the size roast you will need, figure that a standing rib roast typically serves two people per rib. Thus, a four-bone rib roast will serve 8, a 5-bone will serve 10, etc. If the roast seems small to you (perhaps it came from a smaller-framed animal), simply round up what you'll need. You'll always find a use for the leftovers.

Rub the Rosemary Herb rub all over the meat, including the bones. Set it aside at room temperature for about 2 hours.

Preheat the oven to 300°F.

Place the beef, bone-side down, in a roasting pan. Insert a meat thermometer into the rib eye muscle. Roast about 20 minutes per pound, or until the internal temperature is between 120 and 140 degrees.

Remove the meat from the oven and allow it to rest while you prepare the Yorkshire Pudding (recipe follows), and Horseradish Cream.

Yorkshire Pudding

SERVES 6

¼ cup roast beef pan drippings, melted tallow, or butter

3 eqgs, beaten

1 cup whole milk

1 cup flour

1 teaspoon fine salt

Closely related to the popover, Yorkshire Pudding, puffed gloriously high, paired with prime rib and some horseradish cream sauce, is how we define Christmas dinner. It is simple, easy to prepare, dazzling and delicious.

Preheat the oven to 450° F. Pour the pan drippings into a 9-by-9-inch pan, and put it into the oven to keep hot while you prepare the batter. If you don't have enough pan drippings for a full ¼ cup, use tallow or butter to make up the difference.

Whisk together the eggs, milk, flour and salt. Pour the batter into the hot pan and bake 25 minutes or until puffed and golden.

CHAPTER FIVE

Braises, Stews and Soups

When most people think about braises, stews and soups, they imagine a pot of something hearty simmering on the stove on a winter's day. Inevitably, as the days grow colder on the farm sometime around October, our customers begin forsaking grilling steaks and burgers for packages of stew beef, chuck roasts and briskets. But at Sap Bush Hollow we are keenly aware that these cuts have value in the warm months, too. As you will see, I am a big fan of the slow cooker for its energy efficiency, its ability to safely simmer my food while I'm out of the house and can't attend to it, and because it doesn't cause my house to heat up in the dog days of summer. Thus, while most folks are thinking about pot roasts and stews in fall and winter, our family is enjoying them year-round. I hope you will, too.

CHOOSING YOUR POT ROAST

As small farmers, it is impossible for us always to have all cuts of beef in stock. So it is not uncommon for me to witness a wide-eyed customer standing over my meat display whose recipe demands a very specific cut of meat . . . which we don't happen to have in stock. However, if the customer can be flexible, this should hardly ever be a problem, because many cuts of beef are easily interchangeable. As you may have noticed, with most of these recipes, I present a number of cut choice options. The cut you select simply must be suitable for the cooking method. When it comes to braising meat for pot roasts, you will see that there are many cuts to choose from— from **chuck roasts (bone-in or boneless), briskets, short ribs,** or even **bottom round.** They'll all work great, and inevitably, your farmer is bound to have at least one of them in stock. What's important to note is the amount of fat on the cut you choose. **Short ribs**, for instance, will be especially fatty; **briskets** will be more marbled than **chuck,** which, in turn, will definitely be fattier than **bottom round**, one of the leanest cuts on the animal. If your diners are averse to fat, you can predict that they will pick apart their **short ribs** and push aside the luscious buttery, creamy fat, eating just a few morsels of meat. The result is that they'll need more **short ribs** to satisfy their appetite for lean-meat. A **brisket**, because of its marbling, will cook down more than will a **chuck roast** or **bottom round**. When you are estimating portions, you might keep this in mind and select a slightly larger piece of **brisket** than you might ordinarily choose. Another factor to consider is connective tissue. **Bottom round** is lean and has less connective tissue than **brisket** or **chuck,** and thus will cook faster. Because it is significantly leaner, it is also likely to dry out quicker. When calculating the estimated cook times for the following recipes, if you are using a **bottom round**, remember that it will be done on the early side of the time ranges given; **briskets** and **chuck roasts** will be on the long side of the range. But remember: as long as the cut is suitable for braising, it will work with your braising recipe!

A NOTE ABOUT MEAT IN CUBES

I've seen a number of customers get confused when purchasing **stew beef** and **kebabs.** The packages look very similar—cubes of beef wrapped in tight little one- or two-pound packs. While they may look similar, they are not interchangeable. **Kebabs** are usually cut from the sirloin tip, or occasionally from the sirloin. They should be cut into 2-inch cubes, intended for marinating and grilling. To keep them from drying out, they are best served rare or medium rare.

Stew meat is typically cut into 1-inch cubes, taken from the chuck, the brisket, shanks or bottom round. Stew meat will be very chewy if it is grilled. It is meant to be slow-cooked in liquid.

A further distinction that some farmers make is between **bottom round stew** and **chuck, brisket** and **shank stew meat**. Bottom round stew is leaner and contains less connective tissue. Thus, if you need to get a stew made in 90 minutes or less, or if you are fat-averse, bottom round may be your preferred choice. However, cooking bottom round for too long can cause it to dry out. If you are slow-cooking a stew all day, and you prefer a silkier (fattier) texture in your stew meat, the meat cut from the chuck, brisket or shanks will work best.

The Simplest Pot Roast Ever

SERVES 4–10

1 (3–5 pound) beef pot roast, bone-in or boneless (chuck roasts or brisket are ideal)

2 tablespoons coarse salt

1 tablespoon ground black pepper

2 tablespoons lard, butter or tallow

1 cup meat broth

1 large yellow or white onion, sliced in rings

The secret to this recipe is a good sear, followed by time in the slow cooker with very little liquid, resulting in concentrated beef flavor in an intensely robust sauce.

Wipe the roast well with paper towels and rub the salt and pepper into all sides of the meat. Heat a skillet over a medium-high flame, add the fat and swirl to coat. Sear the meat 3–4 minutes per side. Put it in the bottom of a slow cooker. Add the broth to the pan and simmer about 5 minutes, scraping up any browned bits and incorporating them into the juices. When the broth is reduced by about one-third, add it to the slow cooker.

Layer the onion on top of the meat, cover and cook on low 6–8 hours, until tender. Serve the meat with the juice spooned over the top.

Buttermilk Marinated Pot Roast in a Ginger Garlic Chili Sauce

ADVANCE PREPARATION REQUIRED

SERVES 6–8

1 tablespoon coarse salt

2 cups buttermilk, thin yogurt or thick whey*

3–4-pound beef chuck roast (bone in or boneless), short ribs, brisket or bottom round

3 tablespoons lard, butter or tallow

2 medium yellow or white onions, sliced thin

2 teaspoons ground cardamom

1 teaspoon ground coriander

1 teaspoon ground cumin

1 teaspoon chili powder

3 cloves garlic, peeled and crushed

1 tablespoon grated fresh ginger

½ teaspoon ground turmeric

1–2 whole red chipotle peppers, dried

1 tomato, diced

Tired of boring ol' pot roast? Try this fun dish, where Eastern Europe meets India. Eastern Europeans have long marinated their pot roasts in buttermilk, and Indian cuisine often uses yogurt marinades and exotic spices. This recipe draws from both traditions and results in a lightly perfumed beef dish with distinctive yet subtle flavors. We loved this.

Whisk together the salt and buttermilk. Place the beef in a deep-sided glass, stainless-steel, earthenware or other nonreactive dish. Cover with the buttermilk and allow it to marinate overnight in the refrigerator in a covered dish.

Remove the meat from the marinade and pat dry. Reserve the marinade.

Heat 2 tablespoons of the fat in a skillet over a medium-high flame. Add the meat and sear 5 minutes per side. Remove from the pan and place in a slow cooker. If needed, add 1 more tablespoon of fat to the skillet. Add the onions and sauté until clear. Turn the heat down low. Add the cardamom, coriander, cumin, chili powder, garlic, ginger and turmeric. Mix well.

Spread the seasoned onions over the top of the beef in the slow cooker. Add the dried chilies (left whole), diced tomato, and the leftover marinade. Cook on low 6–8 hours until the beef is tender. Remove and discard chilies. Serve the beef with the onions and sauce spooned over the top.

*We make our own yogurt and strain it through cheesecloth so that it is extra-thick. The resulting creamy whey is perfect for this recipe.

Braised Beef in a Cinnamon–Orange Coffee Sauce

ADVANCE PREPARATION REQUIRED

SERVES 6

1 (3–4-pound) bone-in or boneless chuck roast, bottom round roast, short ribs or brisket

2 tablespoons coarse salt

1 tablespoon ground black pepper

3 tablespoons lard, tallow or butter

2 large yellow or white onions, sliced into thin wedges

2 cups strong black coffee

1 cinnamon stick

1 tablespoon honey or maple syrup

2 tablespoons grated orange zest

Here is a mildly sweet and deeply fragrant twist on plain ol' pot roast.

Wipe the meat dry, then rub it all over with salt and pepper. Heat a nonreactive skillet over a medium-high flame, add 2 tablespoons of the fat and swirl to coat. Add the beef and brown it on all sides, about 4 minutes per side. Remove it from the pan and place it on the bottom of a slow cooker.

Lower the heat under the skillet slightly, then add the remaining fat. Once it melts, add the onions. They should sizzle as they hit the pan. If they sputter or splatter, lower the flame. Stir well, coating the onions in the cooking fat and scraping up any browned bits from the bottom of the pan. Continue to cook 2–3 minutes longer until the onions have given up two thirds of their volume in water. Once they start to brown, lower the flame and allow them to caramelize by cooking 15–20 minutes longer, stirring often. Lower the heat if they start to burn.

Pour the onions over the top of the beef in the slow cooker. Return the pan to the flame and add the coffee, cinnamon stick, and honey or maple syrup. Whisk to blend, scraping up any browned bits and incorporating them into the sauce. Bring it to a boil and cook until it is reduced by half. Pour it over the meat, adding the cinnamon stick to the slow cooker as well. Add the orange zest, cover, and cook on low for 6–8 hours until tender. Serve the meat with the onions and sauce spooned over the top.

Slow-Cooker Japanese-Style Curried Beef

SERVES 6–8

4 medium yellow or white onions, thinly sliced

1 clove garlic, minced

2 medium potatoes, unpeeled, cut into 1-inch chunks

5 carrots, unpeeled, cut into 1-inch chunks

¾ cup all-purpose flour, divided

1 tablespoon coarse salt

1 tablespoon freshly ground black pepper

3 tablespoons curry powder, divided use (reduce the amount if you like your food less spicy)

3 pounds stew beef, cubed

7 tablespoons unsalted butter, divided, plus extra, if needed

4 cups canned tomatoes, diced, undrained

2 cups beef broth

2 teaspoons garam masala, lightly toasted, then ground (optional)

When I worked as a schoolteacher in Japan, the cafeteria women prepared enormous stew pots filled with beef curry for our lunches every day throughout the winter. I grew fond of this warming dish, even though Japanese curry is nothing like traditional Thai or Indian curries (I prefer the hot Indian muchi curry from my local co-op). Many folks craving a Japanese-style curry will purchase the ready-made roux mixes from Japanese grocery stores or Asian food markets. I've yet to find this product in the hinterlands of Upstate New York, so the following recipe includes a homemade curry roux that is much better, free from the added sugar, colorings, MSG and other mysterious ingredients of questionable origin found in store-bought mixes. If you are shy with spices, reduce the amount of curry powder or serve it with a generous splash of yogurt. This dish is traditionally served with kimchi, which is a fermented cabbage pickle popular in East Asia.

NOTE: Garam Masala is an Indian spice blend made up of cinnamon, cardamom, cloves, cumin, peppercorns, fennel and bay leaves. It is available whole or already ground in most well-stocked grocery stores, through Indian groceries, or online. To make your own blend, see chapter 8. The recipe will also be successful if you opt to leave it out of the mix.

Layer the onions, garlic, potatoes, and carrots in the bottom of a large slow cooker. Combine ½ cup of the flour, the salt, pepper, and 1 tablespoon of the curry powder in a shallow bowl. Add the beef and toss to coat thoroughly. Heat 3 tablespoons of the butter in a large skillet over medium-high heat. Add the beef and brown on all sides, working in batches and adding more butter if necessary. As it is browned, put the beef on top of the vegetables in the slow cooker. Pour in the tomatoes and beef broth.

Cook on low for 6½ hours (4 hours on high), or until the meat is tender. Stir in the garam masala and allow the stew to continue cooking while you prepare the curry roux.

For the curry roux:

Melt 4 tablespoons butter in a 1-quart saucepan over medium heat. Stir in the remaining ¼ cup flour and 1 to 2 tablespoons of the curry powder (depending on how spicy you like it). Spoon 2 cups liquid from the slow cooker and slowly stir it into the roux. Stir well. Continue to cook and stir until the mixture has thickened, about 2 to 3 minutes. Return the thickened sauce to the cooker and mix well with a wooden spoon.

If you like your sauce thicker, put the slow cooker setting on high and cook 20 to 30 minutes longer with the cover off, stirring often, until the sauce reaches your desired consistency. Serve with rice and a nice helping of kimchi, if you've got it.

LEFTOVERS: Curried beef develops more flavor on the second day. Reheat it in your slow cooker or over low heat on your stove top.

Slow-Cooked Brisket in Beer and Onions

ADVANCE PREPARATION REQUIRED

SERVES 6–8

1 3–4-pound flat-cut brisket

1 tablespoon coarse salt

1 teaspoon ground black pepper

2 tablespoons lard, butter or tallow

4 medium onions, sliced thin

3 tablespoons demi-glace , see Chapter 3, or ½ cup meat broth

1 tablespoon tomato ketchup

12 ounces beer

Here is a recipe for those truly harried days when you can't spend time in the kitchen. Ten minutes of prep time in the morning will have a delicious payoff at suppertime.

Wipe the meat dry with cloth or paper towels and rub the salt and pepper into it. Heat the skillet over a medium–high flame until you see steam coming off of it. Add the fat and swirl to coat. Sear the meat 3–4 minutes per side, then place it on the bottom of a slow cooker. Top with the onions, demi-glace, ketchup, and beer and cook on low, 6–8 hours, until tender.

Slow-Cooked Brisket Hash with Sweet Peppers and Caramelized Onions

SERVES 7–8

1 flat-cut brisket, about 3½ pounds

2 tablespoons coarse salt

1 tablespoon plus 1 teaspoon ground black pepper, divided

6 tablespoons lard, tallow, or butter

1 cup meat broth

4 medium potatoes, unpeeled, diced

1 ½ cups diced roasted red peppers packed in vinegar

3 medium onions, sliced into wedges

1 teaspoon fine salt, or to taste

For topping: 7–16 poached eggs (depending on your company's appetite) and Hollandaise (recipe follows)

Try this recipe for a show-stopping Christmas brunch. Top it with poached eggs and the Hollandaise, and you'll have an unforgettable feast. I guarantee your guests won't be hungry for a good 12 hours or so!

Day before:

Rub the brisket on all sides with salt and 1 tablespoon of the black pepper. Heat a large cast-iron skillet over a medium flame until you can see a little steam coming off it, then add 2 tablespoons of the fat to the pan and swirl to coat. Sear the brisket well, about 2 minutes per side.

Put meat broth into the slow cooker and set the brisket on top. Pour in any remaining pan juices. Cook on low for 5 hours or until meat pulls apart easily. Allow the meat to cool, then use your fingers to shred it into bite-sized pieces. Add it back to the broth and refrigerate.

Day of:

Preheat the oven to 250° F. Remove the meat from the refrigerator and allow it to come to room temperature. Meanwhile, heat a large Dutch oven over a medium flame. Add 2 tablespoons of the fat to the pan and swirl to coat. Add the diced potatoes and sauté until browned. Season with the fine ground salt and remaining pepper, and continue sautéing until tender, about 15 minutes longer. Remove the potatoes and return the Dutch oven to the heat.

Add 2 more tablespoons of the fat to the Dutch oven and swirl to coat. Once it is hot, add the onions. They should sizzle when they hit the pan, but the heat should not be so high that they make a loud sputter. Stir thoroughly, coating the onions with the fat. Continue stirring for 1 minute longer until the onions begin to brown and have lost over half of their volume to water. Lower the flame and cook, stirring often, until they are a deep brown color, about 15 minutes longer.

Add the onions, potatoes, meat and juices, and the roasted red peppers to a large bowl. Mix well and transfer it to a roasting pan. Cover and cook 40 minutes, then remove the cover and cook 20 minutes longer. Serve topped with poached eggs and hollandaise.

Hollandaise Sauce

SERVES 4

8 tablespoons cold butter

4 egg yolks

2 tablespoons lemon juice

1 pinch fine sea salt

1 pinch ground black pepper

I think the single most important sauce to commit to one's memory is the hollandaise. It is the perfect accompaniment for Brussels sprouts, broccoli, cauliflower, poached eggs, hash, even steak, chicken and fish. (I'm sure I've left out other possibilities!) It can turn any simple meal into a stellar feast, rich in beneficial nutrients. Don't be discouraged if your sauce gives you trouble at first. Hollandaise can be fickle, but with a little practice, you will develop a sixth sense about persuading egg yolks to thicken and absorb butter, and you will move through the steps easily, drawing effortlessly on the rescue remedies below to coax the sauce along without giving it a second thought. Before starting, I recommend having a glass of cold water on hand in the event you need some of it for the rescue tip mentioned below (in case the egg yolk gets too hot).

Melt 6 tablespoons of the butter and set aside (keep warm). Cut the remaining butter into small pieces and set next to your stove. Place the egg yolks in a saucepan and whisk vigorously until they have turned lemon yellow and have thickened slightly. Whisk in the lemon juice, salt and pepper, and set the saucepan over a very, very low heat (or, if you prefer, over a double boiler). Whisk the sauce continuously as the egg yolks heat, watching it very carefully. After a few minutes, you will start to see the bottom of the pan show through between your strokes. Promptly remove the egg yolks from the heat and whisk in the cold butter, a few pieces at a time. Once the cold butter has melted into the sauce, slowly drizzle in the melted butter, whisking all the while.

Rescue tips:

If the sauce appears too thin, you have probably not given the egg yolks enough time to cook and thicken. Return the pan to low heat and whisk steadily until it starts to thicken. When you are able to see the pan clearly between your strokes, promptly remove from the heat and add some additional cold butter to the sauce.

If the egg yolks get too hot, the egg will start to cook and the butter will be forced out of suspension, causing the sauce to have a curdled appearance. If this starts to happen, quickly whisk in a tablespoon of ice water, adding additional ice water until the sauce recovers.

If the sauce is too thick, slowly whisk in warm (not hot) water, 1 tablespoon at a time, until it reaches your preferred consistency.

Short Ribs (or Brisket or Shanks) Slow-Cooked with Bacon and Tomatoes

SERVES 6

1 large yellow or white onion, chopped

2 medium carrots, chopped

2 stalks celery, chopped

3–4 pounds beef short ribs, brisket or shanks

1 batch Coriander-Herb Paste (see Chapter 8)

1 tablespoon butter, lard or tallow

3 ounces diced bacon (about 4 thick-cut slices)

2 tablespoons grated lemon zest

½ teaspoon dried thyme (or 1½ teaspoons fresh)

4 cups diced fresh or canned tomatoes

GREMOLATA TOPPING:

3 tablespoons fresh parsley (1 tablespoon dried)

1 tablespoon grated lemon zest

½ cup walnut halves

This is hearty fare that tastes great as a one-dish feast, or stretches farther if poured over a buttery heap of mashed potatoes. There will be a rich, meaty broth when you are finished cooking. If you prefer that your broth have as little grease as possible, use a flat-cut brisket or beef shanks. Leave the short ribs for folks like me, who love the fatty meat!

Place the onions, carrots and celery on the bottom of a large slow cooker. Rub the beef all over with the coriander-herb paste. Heat a skillet over a medium flame and brown the beef, about 4 minutes per side. Set the meat on top of the vegetables in the slow cooker. Add the bacon to the skillet and sauté until lightly browned. Add it to the slow cooker.

Pour ½ cup water into the skillet. Bring it to a simmer, using a wooden spoon to scrape up any browned bits and incorporate them into the pan juices. Pour the pan juices around (not on) the meat in the slow cooker. Add the lemon zest, thyme and tomatoes. Cover and cook on low for 6–8 hours, until tender.

Meanwhile, make the gremolata: combine the parsley, lemon zest and walnuts in the small bowl of a food processor. Process until the nuts are ground. Carve the cooked beef into slices or chunks and serve in shallow bowls, topped with the vegetables, tomatoes and a sprinkling of gremolata.

Stove-Top Stew

SERVES 8–10

3 pounds boneless beef stew meat

3 tablespoons coarse salt, or to taste

1½ tablespoons ground black pepper, or to taste

About 1 tablespoon lard, tallow or butter, or more as needed

2 cups water

2 quarts meat broth

2 cups chopped fresh (preferred) or canned tomatoes

6 medium carrots, cut into bite-size chunks

6 medium boiling potatoes, cut into bite-size chunks

5 medium turnips or parsnips, peeled and cut into bite-size chunks

3 ribs celery, chopped

3 medium onions, sliced into wedges

½ medium-head cauliflower, cut into bite-size pieces

3 cups chopped green beans (or shredded green cabbage)

Okay, okay. I know that cooking a stew in a slow cooker is the most energy-efficient way to do it. But growing up, my dad always made stew in a big pot on the woodstove (and what could be more efficient than cooking with your household heat?), and I just got used to the idea that a good stew was made in large volumes, allowing for multiple meals. I can't get a slow cooker big enough to hold all the stuff I like to put in it (although a scaled-down slow-cooker version of this recipe follows). This is a rather unusual recipe because it calls for relatively few seasonings. Surprisingly, whenever I serve it to guests, they ask me what assortment of exotic spices went into it. When they press me for the secret ingredient, I can only tell them "time." The meat broth simmers for at least two days before I deem it worthy of this stew, concentrating flavor all the while. The vegetables are added at different stages, allowing them to hold onto their inherent flavors and natural texture without sacrificing them to the liquid.

Dry the meat, arrange it on a large platter, and sprinkle with salt and pepper. Heat a large, 8-quart soup pot over a medium–high flame. Add the fat and swirl to coat. Working in small batches so as not to crowd the meat (crowded meat tends to steam rather than brown), brown it on all sides, (about 2 minutes per side). Add more fat if needed.

Once all the meat has browned, return it all to the pot, add the water, and bring it to a simmer, using a wooden spoon to scrape up all the seared-on bits of meat on the bottom of the pan. Once the bottom of the pan is clean and your water is a rich, dark, pan juice, add the broth. Bring to a simmer and lower the heat. Cook on very low heat for 2–3 hours, until the meat is *mostly* (but not *entirely*) tender. Add the tomatoes, carrots, potatoes and turnips, and simmer for 30 minutes longer. By this point the meat should be tender. If not, continue simmering until the meat is fork-tender before proceeding to the final step.

Add the remaining vegetables and cook until the potatoes are easily pierced with a fork and the cauliflower is cooked to your liking, about 20 minutes longer. If you prefer a thicker stew, simmer with the lid off to allow the liquid to cook down.

Serve immediately, or cover and refrigerate and allow the flavors to meld for a day or two before feasting.

Slow-Cooker Stew

SERVES 6

1 medium onion, cut into wedges

3 carrots, cut into bite-sized chunks

2 ribs celery, diced

2 medium boiling potatoes, cut into bite-sized chunks

2 pounds boneless beef stew meat

1½ tablespoons coarse salt

2 teaspoons ground black pepper

About 1 tablespoon lard, butter or tallow, or more as needed

1 quart meat broth

1 cup diced canned tomatoes

2 bay leaves

2 cups green beans, chopped and lightly steamed

Simple. Easy. Tasty. Cooks while you're away. What more is there to say?

Place the onion, carrot, celery, and potatoes on the bottom of a slow cooker. Sprinkle the meat with salt and pepper. Place a skillet over a medium-high flame. Once it has heated through, add the fat and swirl to coat the pan. Working in smaller batches so as not to crowd the meat, brown the cubes well on all sides, about 2 minutes per side. Add additional fat to the pan as needed.

Transfer the meat to the slow cooker. Add the broth, tomatoes, and bay leaves, cover, and cook on low until the meat is fork-tender, about 6 hours. Add the green beans and cook 10 minutes longer, or until they are heated through and done to your liking.

Onion Soup

SERVES 4

2 tablespoons butter

4 large onions, sliced thin into rings

1 cup finely diced cooked beef (optional)

1 teaspoon dried thyme

6 cups meat broth

Coarse salt and ground black pepper to taste

1½ cups grated Swiss, Gruyere, or Cheddar cheese (or a locally-made equivalent)

This recipe is a constant standby in our home. Even when ingredients start to grow slim, there is always enough stuff on hand to make a batch of onion soup, enabling us to create a rich repast from only a few ingredients.

Heat a soup pot over a medium flame. Add the butter, let it melt, and swirl to coat. Add the onions. They should sizzle as they hit the pan; if they sputter or splatter, lower the flame. Stir well, coating the onions in the butter. Continue to cook 2–3 minutes longer, until the onions have given up two-thirds of their volume in water. Once they start to brown, lower the flame and cook, stirring often, until they are caramelized, about 15–20 minutes longer. Lower the heat if they start to burn.

Add the meat (optional), sprinkle in the thyme, and stir well. Pour in the broth and bring to a boil. Lower the flame and simmer until the onions are very tender, about 15–20 minutes longer. Season to taste with salt and pepper. Serve sprinkled with cheese.

Beef Borscht

SERVES 8

2 tablespoons lard, butter or tallow

1 tablespoon coarse salt

2 teaspoons ground black pepper

2 pounds beef shanks, cross-cut 1-inch thick

1 pound red beets, trimmed, peeled, and diced into bite-size pieces

2 medium onions, coarsely chopped

2 medium turnips, peeled and diced into bite-size pieces

2 medium carrots, cut into bite-size pieces

2 cups chopped cabbage (optional)

1/8 teaspoon ground allspice

2 tablespoons tomato paste

4 cloves garlic, crushed

2 quarts meat broth

1 cup sour cream

3 tablespoons dried dill weed

This is a nourishing soup that is inexpensive to make, super-nutritious, and leaves lots of leftovers for subsequent meals. Don't forget to add the sour cream and dill at the end, as they brighten both the flavor and the color.

Heat a large skillet over a medium-high flame. Add the fat and swirl to coat. Dry the beef shanks and rub them with the salt and pepper. Brown them, in batches if necessary, about 4 minutes per side. Set aside. Pour a cup of water into the skillet and bring it to a simmer, stirring and scraping up any browned bits from the pan.

Put the beets, onions, turnips, carrots, and cabbage (if using) into a large slow cooker. Set the browned beef shanks on top. Add the tomato paste, garlic, and broth, cover, and cook on low until the beets are tender and the beef is falling off the bone, about 8 hours. Take up the shanks, let them cool enough to handle, and remove the meat from the bones. Cut it up into bite-sized pieces and return it to the slow cooker. Remove any marrow from the bones and add it back to the slow cooker, discarding the bones. (When no one is looking, I do this by first allowing the bone to cool, then raising one end to my lips like it is a blowgun, and blowing the marrow back into the soup. Anyone with a more hygienic method is welcome to write and tell me about it.) Serve garnished with a generous dollop of sour cream and a sprinkling of dill.

Minestra Maritata

SERVES 8

1 pound ground beef

1 pound ground pork

1½ cups freshly grated Parmesan cheese

1 tablespoon dried oregano or 3 tablespoons finely chopped fresh oregano

1 tablespoon dried parsley or 3 tablespoons finely chopped fresh parsley

2 teaspoons coarse salt

1 teaspoon ground black pepper

2 quarts meat broth

4 cups braising greens (any combination of Swiss chard, cabbage, kale, or collard greens), diced and lightly sautéed

Good-quality extra-virgin olive oil, to taste

The bastardized translation for this recipe is Italian Wedding Soup. No, this soup has nothing to do with Italian weddings. Its American title is the result of a poor translation from the Italian, which celebrates the delicious marriage of meat and vegetables. This soup, another recipe from a glorious but impoverished tradition, allows for myriad variations. Here is the version we enjoy in our home. My daughters love to make the meatballs.

Combine the beef, pork, ½ cup of the Parmesan, the herbs, salt, and pepper in a large bowl. Using your hands, mix well and form into small (½-inch-round) meatballs.

Bring the broth to a boil. Carefully drop in the meatballs. Stir gently to keep them intact, but don't worry if a few break. Cover and simmer until the meatballs rise to the surface, then stir in the braising greens. Simmer a minute longer, until the greens are warmed through.

Serve immediately in shallow bowls topped with the remaining Parmesan and drizzled with olive oil.

"Hearty" Stew with Mashed Potato Dumplings

SERVES 6–8

FOR THE STEW:

1 beef heart

1 pound stew beef (ideally from the chuck), cut into 1-inch cubes

2 tablespoons coarse salt

1 tablespoon ground black pepper

3 tablespoons butter, lard or tallow

1 large onion, thinly sliced

2 cloves garlic, crushed

⅛ teaspoon caraway seeds

1 tablespoon sweet paprika, plus more, for garnish

1 tablespoon hot Hungarian paprika

4 cups meat broth

3 medium tomatoes, diced, or 2 cups diced canned tomatoes

4 medium boiling potatoes, diced

2 carrots, coarsely chopped

1½ cups chopped bell peppers

FOR THE MASHED POTATO DUMPLINGS:

1 cup cold mashed potatoes

½ cup all-purpose flour

1 egg, lightly beaten

1 teaspoon coarse salt

The day I brought a beef heart out of the freezer to write a recipe, my daughter Saoirse became completely fascinated, studying the chambers, the ventricles, etc. We changed the homeschool lesson plan for that morning to accommodate her curiosity. We wound up changing it the next day, too, as she was eager to learn how to cook her science experiment! This stew features beef heart, along with the stew beef, as a way to intensify the meaty richness of the dish. The dumplings just make it plain old fun. And my kids loved it. Yours might, too, if you let them explore the heart and then cook it with you.

Trim any sinew and excess fat from the heart, and remove any blood clots from the ventricles. Slice it in half and clean the inside. Cut it into 1-inch cubes. Combine the heart and stew beef, and season with salt and pepper.

Heat a large, nonreactive (stainless-steel or enameled iron) Dutch oven over a medium-high flame. Add 1 tablespoon of the fat and swirl to coat. Working in small batches, brown the meat well, about 2 minutes per side, adding more fat as needed. Add the remaining fat and onions and sauté, stirring often, until they are caramelized, about 15 minutes.

In a small bowl, use a fork to mash together the garlic, caraway seeds, and both paprikas, and stir it into the onions.

Return the meat to the pot and pour in the broth. Bring to a simmer, cover, and reduce the heat. Simmer 1 hour or until the meat is very tender. Add the tomatoes and potatoes, and simmer 30 minutes longer. Add the carrots and peppers and simmer until the carrots are crisp-tender, about 10–15 minutes longer.

In a medium mixing bowl, combine the mashed potatoes, egg, flour and salt, and mix well, then roll it into 1-inch-round balls.

Drop the dumplings into the simmering stew and cook until they float to the surface, about 15 minutes. Sprinkle with paprika and serve.

Tongue Confit

SERVES 4

1 cup coarse sea salt

2 teaspoons crumbled dried thyme

2 teaspoons ground black pepper

1 beef tongue

4-5 cups lard, duck or goose fat

Grainy or Dijon mustard, for serving

For surviving the chaotic throes of the growing season, I am forever seeking ways to have nutritious, cold meats on hand that make for easy on-the-go lunches and snacks, without having to succumb to plain 'ol cold cuts. Confits have historically been a way to preserve meats for months on end. However, for them to work properly, the stored meats must be cooked and covered in fat. Duck or goose fat is the traditional choice for such a project, but since most of us find it easier to have lard on hand than goose or duck fat, I've written this recipe for lard. If you have the good fortune of having goose or duck fat, use it!

P.S. My girls really enjoyed watching me prepare this (especially the part where I peeled the tongue). And, after watching, they really enjoyed eating it.

Combine the salt, thyme and black pepper in a deep glass baking dish. Pour this out on a cutting board. Lay the tongue on the salt, then roll it around until is is thoroughly coated and buried in salt. Seal in the container and refrigerate overnight.

On the day you are ready to cook it, preheat the oven to 200° F. Remove the tongue from the salt, rinse, and blot dry, then place it in a nonreactive stainless-steel or enameled iron Dutch oven or other heavy-bottomed flameproof pot. Cover with fat and bring it to a simmer over direct medium-high heat. If, once the fat melts, the tongue is not completely submerged, add more fat until it is completely submerged.

Bring the fat to a gentle simmer, cover, and bake gently until the tongue is tender, about 4–6 hours (lamb and pork tongues will cook faster than beef).

Alternatively, simply put the tongue in a slow cooker, and cook on low, making sure it is completely covered in fat, for 6-8 hours, or until it is tender.

Using tongs, lift the tongue from the fat, let cool enough to handle, and carefully peel the skin. Set the tongue in an earthenware crock (or any container that will keep the light out). Pour the hot cooking fat on top, let cool, and refrigerate. Once it is completely cooled and the fat has congealed, seal the container tightly. It will be ready to eat the next day, but is better if allowed to ripen for a week. Tongue Confit will keep, covered and refrigerated, for up to six months. Serve cold, sliced thin and accompanied by grainy or Dijon mustard.

A NOTE TO THE FRUGAL: The fat that you use for this confit can be reused, either when sautéing or for another confit. Since it will be flavored by the herbs and salt, be mindful that whatever dish you choose to use it in is compatible with the preseasoned fat. After a few uses in confit, it will become quite salty and you will want to start with a fresh batch once more.

Corned Beef Tongue with Horseradish Cream and Grainy Mustard

SERVES 6

2 quarts water

1 12-ounce bottle beer

1 ½ cups coarse salt

3 tablespoons pickling spices

5 bay leaves

1 cup granulated maple sugar, sucanat, or turbinado sugar

1 large or 2 small beef tongues

1 large onion, coarsely chopped

6 whole allspice berries

½ teaspoon whole black peppercorns

1 whole star anise

1 cup sour cream

4 teaspoons bottled horseradish, or more, to taste

Crackers, 1 baguette, thinly sliced, or 1–2 sliced cucumbers

Grainy mustard

Anyone who has ever disdained trying tongue must have forgotten that he or she has one in their mouth all the time. OK. OK. Maybe that's a bit off-color for this recipe . . . but the joke was as irresistible as this simple recipe, which will make tongue-lovers out of even the greatest skeptics. Since the tongue is brined, begin the initial (and very easy) prep work at least a week before you plan to eat it.

It can be served with crackers, baguette, or sliced cucumber, as given here, but is also delicious served as a traditional corned beef dinner, paired with cabbage and potatoes simmered in the cooking liquid.

Put the water, beer, salt, pickling spices, 3 bay leaves, and sugar into a soup pot. Bring to a boil and simmer until the sugar and salt are dissolved. Pour this into a stainless-steel or other heatproof, nonreactive container and let it cool.

Add the tongue, cover, and refrigerate 7 days, turning every few days.

On the morning of the 7th day, drain the tongue, discarding the brine. Set the tongue on the bottom of a slow cooker. Add the onion, 2 bay leaves, allspice, peppercorns, and star anise. Completely cover with water (at least 1 quart) and turn on the heat to low. Bring slowly to a simmer and cook gently until the skin of the tongue peels easily and the flesh pierces easily with a fork, about 8–10 hours.

Remove it from the cooking liquid and allow it to cool enough to handle. Peel the skin and slice thinly.

Mix together the sour cream and horseradish in a small bowl. Season to taste with additional horseradish, if necessary.

Serve hot or cold with crackers, sliced baguette, on cucumber slices, or alone, garnished with a dollop of your choice of horseradish cream or grainy mustard.

LEFTOVERS: Corned tongue makes great grilled Rueben sandwiches garnished with sauerkraut, Swiss cheese, and a little Russian dressing, or serve it cold on pumpernickel bread with tomato, mustard and capers. I like to make a platter with cold tongue, horseradish cream, mustard, pickled beets, dilly beans and a nice, sharp, raw cheddar.

Salsa Soup with Meatballs and Oxtails

SERVES 6

1 tablespoon coarse salt, plus
   1 teaspoon, finely ground

3 teaspoons ground black pepper

2 pounds oxtails

2 tablespoons butter or lard

1 tablespoon olive oil

4 cloves garlic, minced

1 jalapeno chili, seeds and membrane
   removed, diced

2 medium onions, diced

2 medium carrots, diced

4 cups canned chopped tomatoes, with
   their juices

4 cups meat broth

1 teaspoon smoked paprika

1 pound ground beef

½ teaspoon ground cumin

½ cup chopped fresh cilantro

½ cup long grain rice

While this mixed-meat dish can be made with ordinary stew beef as a substitute for oxtails, these gelatinous-rich delights lend a lovely unctuous quality that balances the brightness of the salsa soup base.

Combine the coarse salt and 2 teaspoons pepper, and sprinkle it over the surface of the oxtails. Heat a large, nonreactive stainless-steel or enameled iron Dutch oven over a medium-high flame. Add 2 tablespoons of the fat and swirl to coat. Add the oxtails and sear 2–3 minutes per side, taking care to ensure that, as you brown the meat, there is about 1 inch of space around every piece (work in batches if necessary). Remove the oxtails to a separate dish.

Lower the heat. Add the olive oil to the pot and swirl to coat. Add the garlic, jalapeno, onions, and carrots, and sauté until the onions are translucent, stirring often to scrape up any browned bits. Pour in the tomatoes and broth and add the paprika. Return the oxtails to the sauce, cover, and simmer gently 1 ½ hours.

Meanwhile, combine the ground meat, ground salt, 1 teaspoon pepper, cumin and ¼ cup of cilantro in a bowl. Mix well and form into 1-inch balls.

Once the oxtails have simmered about 1½ hours, add the rice, if using. Simmer 45 minutes, then add the meatballs and simmer until they float in the broth and the rice is tender, about 15–20 minutes longer.

Serve in shallow bowls to unfussy dinner companions who will delight in sucking the bits of meat off the oxtail bones, garnished with the remaining cilantro. Consider offering small side plates as bone repositories.

CHAPTER SIX

Ground Beef

When a new customer approaches my farmers market stall seeking their first grassfed experience, I nearly always send them home with a package of ground beef. I do this for several reasons. First, it is the easiest and most familiar meat on the animal to cook. Any recipe that you have for ground beef at home will work with what your grassfed farmer is selling you at the market. Second, because grassfed ground beef is taken from the parts of the animal that do the most work and build up the most connective tissue, it is probably the most flavorful cut of meat that a grass farmer can sell. New customers will immediately notice the taste difference, without having to learn how to properly grill a steak. And finally, it is our least expensive cut of meat. When transitioning over to a new way of eating meat, I'd prefer that customers experiment with an inexpensive cut first.

It is rare for a grass farmer to be sold out of ground beef. It is our most bountiful cut, and one of my favorites. At least once a week, I find myself craving a grassfed burger. I serve it just as I would a good steak —without a bun, and topped with nothing more than a little pat of herbed butter. Ketchup never comes to our table for burgers . . . there is too much glorious flavor to warrant drowning the meat in sugary-sweet tomato schlop.

The best part of ground beef is its versatility. It can be a flavorful, inexpensive roast when patted into a meatloaf, a comforting meat pie, an elegant hors-d'oeuvre. The choices are seemingly endless, and the flavor is always rewarding.

Cornish Pasties

SERVES 4

For the crust:

2 cups flour

1 teaspoon fine salt

6 ounces minced tallow

½ cup cold water

Flour to dust the work surface

For the filling:

1 pound ground beef

1 medium onion, finely chopped

1 small turnip, peeled and diced

2 medium potatoes, diced

2 medium carrots, diced

2 teaspoons dried thyme

2 teaspoons dried parsley

1½ teaspoons salt

1 teaspoon ground black pepper

Milk to brush the pasties

While learning about the California Gold Rush, the girls and I explored some of the food the miners would have eaten. In the early 1850s, hundreds of men from Cornwall England arrived in California, their experience with hard-rock and deep-shaft mining being in demand. They brought with them their taste for meat pies, and the Cornish Pasty found its way to the United States. When they lunched on their pasties down in the mines, legend has it they always left a bite for the Tommyknockers, the spirits of departed miners, in hopes they'd help keep them safe during their dangerous work. While leaving an unfinished bite might be wise, I will attest to the fact that it can require an awful lot of willpower . . .

Blend the flour and salt in a mixing bowl. Add the tallow and use a pastry cutter or fork to cut it into the flour until the texture is similar to cornmeal. Add water and mix. Turn dough out onto a floured surface and knead for a few seconds until soft and not sticky. Divide into four balls, place in an airtight container and refrigerate for 2 hours.

Preheat the oven to 375°F.

Mix together the ground beef, vegetables, herbs, salt and pepper. Remove the dough from the refrigerator. Working on a floured surface, roll each ball into an 8-inch circle. Brush the edges of each circle with milk. Place 1 cup of filling on one half of each circle and fold the other half over it. Seal the edges by pressing with a fork.

Transfer each pasty to a greased cookie sheet. Cut 3–4½-inch slits in the top of each pasty to let out steam. Brush the surface with milk, then bake for 45 minutes, or until golden brown.

Shepherd's Pie

SERVES 6

For the mashed-potato topping:

2 pounds coarsely chopped potatoes

4 tablespoons unsalted butter

½ cup whole milk or cream

1 clove garlic, minced

½ teaspoon coarse salt

½ teaspoon ground pepper

For the filling:

2 tablespoons unsalted butter, lard, or olive oil, plus more if needed

2 medium onions, diced

4 medium carrots, diced

2 cups green beans, coarsely chopped

1 cup corn (or peas, or a combination of both)

2 pounds ground beef

1½ teaspoons coarse salt, plus more to taste

1 teaspoon freshly ground pepper, plus more to taste

⅓ cup all-purpose flour (or 3 tablespoons arrowroot whisked into 3 tablespoons ice water)

1 quart meat broth

4 ounces freshly grated Parmesan cheese

This one is a favorite in our house. It is simple, comforting, nourishing, flavorful, and we all clamor for the leftovers.

Put the potatoes in a pot of water to cover and bring to a boil. Cook until tender and drain off all the water. Alternatively, put the potatoes in a pressure cooker with 8 ounces of water and cook for 7 minutes at 15 psi. Allow the pressure to subside using the natural release method, following the manufacturer's directions. Strain off the water.

Put the potatoes in a large bowl. Add the butter, milk, garlic, salt, pepper, and smash thoroughly until smooth. Set aside.

Preheat the oven to 350° F.

Place a large ovenproof casserole over medium heat. Add the butter and onions, carrots, green beans and any other vegetables you choose. Sauté until the onions are clear and the vegetables crisp-tender, about 7 minutes. Remove all to a separate bowl.

Crumble the ground beef and add to the casserole, season with the salt and pepper (add more fat to the pot if needed), and sauté until browned. Sprinkle in the flour and slowly stir in the broth. (If using arrowroot and water, add it now.) Bring the mixture to a boil, stirring often, and then reduce it to a simmer and cook until thickened. Return the vegetables to the casserole, stir well, and taste for salt and pepper.

Remove the casserole from the heat. Spread the mashed potatoes over the top, sprinkle with the parmesan cheese and bake until the surface of the potato topping is lightly browned, about 30 to 45 minutes.

Simple Meat Loaf

SERVES 6

4 tablespoons unsalted butter or lard

1 medium onion, diced

1 pound ground beef

1 pound bulk pork sausage (sweet Italian, hot Italian, bratwurst, or kielbasa all work well), or one pound ground veal, or one more pound of ground beef

1 teaspoon coarse salt

1 teaspoon ground black pepper

Meat loaf has noble, albeit humble, origins back to the days of meat scarcity, when bread crumbs or oatmeal made a little ground beef go a long way. Were I to be faithful to this tradition, I'd have written a recipe that included the extra starch, but I just never liked it cooked that way. I want my meat loaf to be made of meat, and to be so simple that I never have to look up a recipe for it. With only four ingredients plus salt and pepper, I think this is the best version you'll ever taste. It's every bit as homey as what your grandmother fixed, but not as mealy.

Preheat the oven to 350° F.

Melt the butter in a sauté pan over medium heat. Add the onion and sauté until translucent. Turn off the heat and allow the onion to cool. Place the beef and sausage in a bowl. Add the salt, pepper, and butter-onion mixture. Using your hands, mix well, but lightly; press meat into a 9-inch loaf pan. Roast 1 hour. Serve immediately, spooning any pan juices on top of the meat.

Garlic and Olive Meatballs with Braised Vegetables

SERVES 6–8

1 pound ground pork, ground veal or loose sweet Italian or hot Italian sausage

1 pound ground beef

2 hard-boiled eggs, finely diced

1 cup green olives, pitted and diced

3 cloves garlic, minced

5 tablespoons dried parsley, divided use

About 1 teaspoon fine salt (to taste)

About 1 teaspoon ground black pepper (to taste)

4 tablespoons lard, tallow or butter

2 medium fennel bulbs, cut into ¼-inch-thick wedges

6 carrots, cut diagonally into ½-inch pieces

2 medium turnips, peeled and diced into ½-inch pieces

3 cups meat broth

2 tablespoons cold water

1 tablespoon arrowroot

Ground beef is some of the most flavorful meat that comes off a grassfed steer or cow. While it is wonderful to enjoy it as a deeply satisfying burger, it seems a pity not to let it play a part in more sophisticated fare. Recipe test note: My kids loved these meatballs (they love anything with olives), and they liked the fennel and carrots. They weren't so keen on the turnips . . . but we grown-ups sure enjoyed them!

Place the ground meat in a large bowl. Add the diced eggs, ¾ cup of the olives, the garlic, parsley, and salt and pepper to taste. Using your hands, mix well, then shape into 1½-inch-diameter balls.

Position a rack 4–6 inches below the heat source and preheat the oven broiler. Rub a large cast-iron skillet or baking sheet with 1 tablespoon of the fat. Line up meatballs on the pan, allowing at least 1 inch space around each ball (you may need to do multiple batches). Broil 4–6 inches from the heat for 5 minutes, use tongs to turn them over, and broil 5 minutes longer.

While meatballs are broiling, heat 1 tablespoon of the fat over medium-high heat in a large Dutch oven or 8-quart soup pot. Working in small batches so as not to crowd your pan, brown all the vegetables, about 4 minutes per batch. Remove vegetables to a bowl after browning each batch, and add more fat as needed.

Once all the vegetables are browned, return them all to the Dutch oven. Set the meatballs on top and pour in the broth. Cover and simmer until the vegetables are tender, about 15–20 minutes. Using a slotted spoon, remove the vegetables and meatballs to a large serving bowl. Leave the broth simmering in the pot.

In a small bowl, whisk together the arrowroot and cold water. Pour the mixture into the Dutch oven and gently stir until the sauce is slightly thickened. Remove from the heat, pour over the vegetables and meatballs and serve, garnished with the remaining parsley and olives.

Stuffed Chard with Lemon Cream Sauce

10–12 large Swiss chard leaves, stems removed

1 egg, beaten

1 pound ground beef, veal, pork or lamb

2 cups finely shredded cabbage

1 tablespoon chopped fresh dill leaves (or 1 teaspoon dried)

2 teaspoons grated lemon zest

½ teaspoon ground allspice

1 teaspoon fine salt

1 teaspoon ground black pepper

2 tablespoons butter

1 clove garlic, crushed

2 cups meat broth

1 cup sour cream or heavy cream

2 tablespoons lemon juice

Here is a clever (and tasty) way to convert humble ingredients like greens, cabbage and ground beef into stylish fare.

Remove the stems from the greens and discard. Place the leaves in a large heatproof bowl and cover with boiling water. After 5 minutes, strain off the water, lay the leaves out on a towel and pat dry.

Combine the egg, ground meat, cabbage, dill, lemon zest, allspice, salt and pepper in a bowl. Mix well. Scoop up meat and cabbage mixture by quarter cupfuls, shape into cylinders and set each cylinder at the stem end of each leaf. Roll up, tucking the sides as you go to form a bundle.

Heat a large, nonreactive skillet over a medium flame. Add the butter and swirl to coat. Place the stuffed greens in the skillet seam-side down. Whisk the crushed garlic into the broth, then pour it into the skillet. Bring the broth to a light simmer, reduce heat, cover, and cook 30 minutes.

Remove the greens to a serving platter using a slotted spoon. Increase the heat in the skillet and simmer the broth down until it is reduced by two-thirds. Whisk in the sour cream, then the lemon juice. Season to taste with salt and pepper. Pour over the stuffed greens and serve.

Oven Roasted Burgers with Garlic-Chive Goat Cheese

SERVES 4

For the Garlic-Chive Goat Cheese

4 ounces goat cheese

2 teaspoons fine salt, divided use

3 tablespoons olive oil

1 teaspoon granulated garlic

2 tablespoons minced fresh chives or green onions, or 2 teaspoons dried chives

1 pound ground beef

1 teaspoon ground black pepper

2 tablespoons tallow, lard, or butter

Here is another family-favorite, a delightful way to enjoy a rich beefy burger, even if I don't feel like trudging out to the grill midwinter.

NOTE: This recipe is for cooking a burger indoors. If you would like to cook burgers out on the grill, see the recipe for Grilled Burgers in Chapter 7.

Place the goat cheese, 1 teaspoon salt, olive oil, granulated garlic, and chives in a small dish. Use a fork to smash it all together and thoroughly mix it. Set it aside.

Preheat the oven to 200° F.

Combine the ground beef with the remaining salt and pepper. Loosely shape the meat into four balls. Gently flatten them until they are about 1 inch thick. With your fingertips, make a small well in the top of each patty to prevent them from swelling.

Place a large ovenproof skillet over a high flame. When you begin to see a little smoke rising off the skillet, add the fat, swirl to coat, then add the burgers. Make sure there is about 1 inch of space around each burger as it sears in the pan. Sear the burgers for 4 minutes on each side.

Transfer the pan to the oven. Roast 10 minutes, then serve topped with the garlic-chive goat cheese.

Oven Roasted Breakfast Burgers

SERVES 4

1 pound ground beef

1 teaspoon fine salt

1 teaspoon ground black pepper

2 teaspoons dried thyme

3 ounces finely diced uncooked bacon

2 tablespoons lard, tallow or butter

NOTE: The follow recipe is for cooking a burger indoors. If you would like to cook burgers out on the grill, see the recipe for Grilled Burgers in Chapter 7.

Yup. You read the title right. Burgers for breakfast. Why not? It can't be eggs every day, you know. Meat for breakfast, beyond the typical bacon, ham and sausage routine is an old farm tradition.

Preheat the oven to 200° F.

Combine the ground beef with the salt, pepper, thyme and bacon. Loosely shape the meat into four balls. Gently flatten them until they are about 1 inch thick. With your fingertips, make a small well in the top of each patty to prevent them from swelling.

Place a large ovenproof skillet over a high flame. When you begin to see a little smoke rising off the skillet, add the fat, swirl to coat, then add the burgers. Make sure there is about 1 inch of space around each burger as it sears in the pan. Sear the burgers for 4 minutes on each side.

Transfer the pan to the oven and roast 10 minutes longer.

WELL-DONE BURGERS AND RAW MEAT

Okay, if you've been paying attention, you are probably aware of my opinion that meat should never be cooked beyond medium-rare, unless it is a pot roast or stew. There is one other exception: burgers.

When we grind beef in the cutting room, we make it from all the good-quality scraps of meat we can salvage, in an effort to prevent waste. Some of the meat and fat is meat from the exterior of the carcass, some of it from the interior. Exterior meat does have a greater chance of carrying potentially harmful pathogens, such as *E.coli*. Although *E.coli* is less prevalent on grassfed beef, and the strain of *E.coli* found in grassfed is usually one that our stomach acids can easily destroy, I prefer to play it safe with my burger-cooking recommendations. If *E.coli* is located on the exterior surface of a steak, it is almost always killed in the cooking process. But when the exterior meat is blended with the interior meat, which happens with ground beef, some of it will be inside your burger, and some of it will be on the outside. While pathogens on the exterior will be killed upon exposure to the heat, the inside of the burger, if left rare, can still harbor the little vectors of illness, *if the beef was tainted.* For that reason, I recommend searing burgers over high heat, then finishing them indirectly on the grill, or in the oven. The sear helps prevent drying out the burger while the extra cooking time helps ensure that the meat is cooked through. Better still, it gives the sugars an opportunity to caramelize over the surface of the burger, giving it a glossy finish and delicious flavor.

That said, if you like a rare burger, I think choosing local, grassfed beef is your safest bet. The same is true if you like steak carpaccio, kibbeh (raw ground lamb), or steak tartare. My family has happily eaten these raw dishes repeatedly, with no ill effects. However, it is important to be aware of the risks when choosing to eat these foods. If you are curious about what raw meat tastes like, but are not keen on taking any risks with food-borne pathogens, try the Steak Carpaccio. Instead of serving it raw, simply sear the steak briefly over high heat before chilling it and slicing it.

Stuffed Peppers

SERVES 4

2 tablespoons olive oil, butter, lard or tallow

1 medium onion, finely minced

1 clove garlic, minced

2 cups finely shredded cabbage

1 pound ground beef, or 1–2 cups finely minced leftover beef

1 teaspoon dried thyme (or 1 tablespoon fresh)

1 teaspoon dried oregano (or 1 tablespoon fresh)

1 teaspoon dried basil (or 1 tablespoon fresh)

Coarse salt and ground black pepper, to taste

1 cup tomato sauce or 2 diced fresh tomatoes

4 whole medium sweet peppers, cut in half lengthwise, seeds and membranes removed

8 ounces whole-milk mozzarella cheese, or any other easy-melting cheese, sliced thin

I love simple and satisfying rustic fare like this, which celebrates late summer's bounty. We also cut a few peppers in half each fall to put in the freezer to have them ready for this meal come winter.

Preheat the oven to 350° F. Heat the fat in a large skillet over medium heat. Add the onions and sauté until clear, about 4 minutes. Add the garlic and sauté a minute longer, taking care to control the heat so as not to scorch it. Stir in the cabbage and sauté until crisp-tender. Stir in the meat. If you are working with leftover cooked meat, sauté just until the ingredients are heated through. If you are working with fresh ground meat, sauté about 5–7 minutes until the meat is browned. Stir in the herbs, then season to taste with salt and pepper. Stir in the tomato sauce. Stuff each pepper half with the filling, top with cheese, place in a casserole dish and bake 25 minutes.

Kid alternative: A giant half pepper can be a bit cumbersome for little fingers and mouths. If you need to cook for little ones, I suggest following all the directions as above. Then, instead of filling the bell pepper halves, dice them finely and stir them into the cabbage and meat. Put all the ingredients into a casserole dish, top with cheese, and bake at 350 degrees for 20 minutes. This was extremely popular with my little ones!

73

Hearty Macaroni and Cheese

SERVES 6

1 tablespoon olive oil

9 ounces dry pasta (elbow, fusilli, or ziti all work)

2 tablespoons lard, olive oil, butter or tallow

1 medium onion, finely diced

2½ cups broccoli (fresh or frozen), diced

1 pound ground beef , OR 2–3 cups finely diced leftover cooked meat

½ cup sundried tomatoes, diced

1 cup grated cheddar cheese

1 cup grated whole-milk mozzarella cheese

½ cup grated parmesan cheese

1 cup heavy cream

3 eggs

½ teaspoon cayenne pepper

1 teaspoon salt

1 teaspoon ground black pepper

4 tablespoons butter

1 cup bread crumbs

Okay, one look at this recipe and you'll realize that I am no wimp when it comes to the butterfat. This dish is so rich and creamy that a little goes a long way. If you are not able to tolerate so much butterfat, feel free to substitute milk for the cream. Leftovers are even tastier the next day.

Preheat the oven to 350°F. Lightly grease a 9-by-12-inch baking pan or casserole dish. Bring 4 quarts water to a rolling boil over high heat. Add the olive oil and stir in the pasta. Cook until just al dente. Drain and arrange it on the bottom of the prepared pan. Melt the remaining fat in a large skillet and put in the onions and broccoli. Sauté until the onions are clear and the broccoli is crisp-tender. Add the meat and continue to sauté until it is cooked through. Sprinkle this on top of the pasta. Scatter the sundried tomatoes on top, then layer the cheddar, mozzarella and parmesan over everything. In a separate bowl, whisk together the cream, eggs, cayenne, salt and pepper. Pour it over the casserole. Melt the butter in a small saucepan over a medium flame, mix in the crumbs, then scatter them over the top of the casserole. Bake 40 minutes, or until bubbly and lightly browned on top.

74

Moussaka

SERVES 8

5 tablespoons lard or butter, or
   3 tablespoons lard or butter and
   2 tablespoons olive oil

2 medium onions, diced

2 cloves garlic, minced

2 pounds ground beef

2 cups diced fresh or canned tomatoes

1 cup meat broth

¼ cup chopped fresh parsley or
   1 tablespoon dried

1 tablespoon chopped fresh oregano or
   1 teaspoon dried

½ teaspoon ground cinnamon

5 tablespoons flour

2 cups heavy cream (or milk)

3 eggs, beaten

Coarse salt and ground black pepper

1 cup grated Parmesan cheese

2 eggplants (about 1¼ pounds each),
   peeled and sliced into thin rounds

This easy-to-prepare one-dish dinner takes advantage of the summer harvest while repurposing your leftover meats into a tasty repast.

Preheat oven to 350°F. Heat 2 tablespoons of the fat or olive oil, if using, in a large skillet over a medium flame. Add the onions and sauté until clear, then stir in the garlic. Sauté 1 minute longer and stir in the meat, tomatoes, broth, herbs and cinnamon. Set aside.

Heat the remaining fat in a saucepan over medium heat. When the foaming subsides, blend in the flour until smooth, and stir until lightly browned, about a minute. Slowly whisk in the cream, bring to a simmer, and cook 3–5 minutes, until slightly thickened. Slowly whisk a quarter cup of the hot sauce into the eggs, then stir them back into the sauce. Bring to a simmer, whisking constantly, and simmer until thick and creamy. Turn off the heat, season to taste with salt and pepper, and stir in half of the Parmesan.

Lightly grease a 9-by-13-inch glass baking dish and arrange half the eggplant on the bottom. Sprinkle with salt and pepper, then top with all of the meat sauce.

Arrange the remaining eggplant over the top, then pour the custard evenly over it and smooth it with a spatula. Sprinkle evenly with the remaining Parmesan. Cover and bake 1 hour, then remove the cover and bake until the top has lightly browned, about 10–15 minutes longer.

Summer Harvest Casserole

SERVES 8

3 medium eggplants, peeled and sliced into ¼-inch-thick rounds

Olive oil

3 tablespoons butter, lard, or tallow (or use all olive oil)

1 medium onion, coarsely chopped

2 medium carrots, diced

1 clove garlic, minced

1–2 pounds ground beef

6 medium fresh tomatoes, diced

1 tablespoon chopped fresh basil, or 1 teaspoon dried basil

1 tablespoon chopped fresh oregano, or 1 teaspoon dried oregano

1 teaspoon coarse salt

Ground black pepper, to taste

1 pound whole-milk ricotta cheese

2 tablespoons diced fresh chives

1 egg, beaten

8 ounces goat cheese

1 cup freshly grated Parmesan

This one-dish dinner is perfectly suited for a late-summer meal, as it makes use of many of the vegetables spilling out of the garden.

Preheat broiler. Brush both sides of the eggplant rounds with olive oil, then place on a baking sheet. Broil, turning once, until lightly browned on both sides (about 2 minutes per side) and set aside to cool.

Heat the fat in a large nonreactive (stainless-steel or enameled) skillet over medium heat. Add the onion, carrots and garlic, and sauté until the onions are clear. Add the meat and cook until it is lightly browned, stirring often to break up any clumps. Add the tomatoes, basil, oregano, salt, and pepper to taste. Lower the heat, cover, and simmer 10 minutes. Remove the lid and simmer until the sauce has thickened, about 30 minutes longer.

Preheat oven to 350° F. Lightly grease a 9-by-13-inch baking dish. Spoon in enough meat sauce to coat the bottom, and spread it evenly. Cover with half the eggplant rounds. In a separate bowl, mix together the ricotta, egg, and chives, and spread it evenly over the eggplant. Lay the remaining eggplant over the ricotta, sprinkle with the goat cheese, and top with the remaining meat sauce. Sprinkle the Parmesan evenly over the top, cover, and bake 30 minutes. Uncover and bake until the sauce is bubbling and the cheese is lightly browned, about 10–15 minutes longer.

Parmesan–Cheddar One-Crust Meat Pie

SERVES 6

6 tablespoons lard or butter

2 cups diced fresh or leftover vegetables (onions, green peppers, carrots, peas, corn, or green beans . . . even lima beans, will all work)

2 tablespoons all-purpose flour or arrowroot

2 cups meat broth

¼ teaspoon mace

¼ teaspoon crumbled dried rosemary, or ¾ teaspoon chopped fresh rosemary

Coarse salt and ground black pepper, to taste

1 pound ground beef, or 2 cups diced leftover beef

Parmesan-Cheddar Pie Crust (see recipe below)

1 egg yolk beaten with 1 tablespoon water

This is a hearty meal, and is even better when reheated on a second day and served with a wedge of extra-sharp cheddar.

NOTE: for those of you averse to using wheat flour, you can top the pie with potatoes mashed with liberal amounts of butter, then sprinkle the topping with Parmesan or cheddar cheese. The flour in the meat sauce can be replaced with potato flour.

Preheat the oven to 450° F. Heat 2 tablespoons of the fat in a skillet over a medium flame. Add the fresh vegetables and sauté until crisp-tender. Add in any leftover vegetables, if using, and continue sautéing until they are just warmed through. Remove them from the pan and set aside. Add the remaining fat. Heat, stirring constantly, until the butter has melted and is no longer foaming. Sprinkle the flour on top and whisk thoroughly until a paste forms. Slowly stir in the meat stock and bring to a boil, stirring constantly. Reduce the flame intensity and simmer until the sauce is thick, about 7 minutes. Mix in the mace, rosemary, salt and pepper. Stir in the meat and the vegetables, then pour into a 10-inch, deep-pie dish or 9-inch-square baking pan. Roll out the pie crust on a floured surface ¼-inch thick, then carefully lay it over the top of the filling. Don't fret if the crust crumbles. Just work it back together and slide it on top. Crimp the edges, then poke a few holes on the surface. Brush the crust with the yolk and water mixture, and bake until the crust is lightly browned, about 20–25 minutes.

Parmesan Cheddar Pie Crust

1 cup all-purpose flour

1/2 teaspoon coarse salt

½ teaspoon ground black pepper

⅛ teaspoon baking powder

¼ pound (one stick) cold butter, diced

¾ cup grated cheddar

½ cup grated Parmesan cheese

¼ cup ground walnuts

I often double this recipe, then store the extra crust in the freezer for another use.

Combine the flour, salt, pepper, and baking powder. Using a pastry cutter or fork, blend in the butter until the mixture resembles coarse meal. Using your hands, thoroughly mix in the cheese and nuts until the dough forms a solid ball. Chill until ready to use, but allow it to soften at room temperature before rolling it out.

Unlike a conventional pie crust, this dough will be more crumbly and will require your forbearance if it breaks when you lift it over the pie. Simply push the broken pieces together and move forward. The extraordinary flavor and texture will make it well worth any cosmetic imperfections.

Slow-Cooker Chili

SERVES 6

For the chili:

1 pound dried dark red kidney beans

2 tablespoons fresh lemon juice

1 pound ground beef

2 tablespoons olive oil

1 dried ancho chili pepper, seeds and
white membrane removed, chopped

1 dried whole chipotle pepper

1 medium onion, coarsely chopped

1 28-ounce can crushed tomatoes

2 cloves garlic, chopped

2 tablespoons chili powder

1 teaspoon freshly ground cumin

1 teaspoon dried oregano

1 teaspoon salt

1 teaspoon freshly ground

black pepper

For the topping:

1 cup shredded Monterey Jack
or cheddar cheese

1 cup sour cream

The secret to chili is how you select and use your chili peppers. If dried ancho and chipotle peppers are not available in your local market, just substitute, bearing these points in mind: dried chiles have a richer, fruitier flavor than fresh; smaller chiles are hotter than larger ones; the seeds and white veins generally contain all the heat but no chili flavor; and finally, if you like great chili flavor but are less enamored with the spicey heat, add one whole chili pepper to the pot, but remove it before serving. The recipe below is for a medium-hot chili.

Cover beans with warm water, stir in lemon juice, cover, and soak in a warm place for 18 to 24 hours. Drain, rinse, and place in a slow cooker.

In a skillet over medium-low heat, brown the ground beef in olive oil. Combine the meat and remaining chili ingredients in the slow cooker, and cook on high for 4 to 5 hours or on low for 8 to 10 hours, until the beans are tender. Depending on how your cooker works, you may need to add an extra ½ cup of water during the cooking time to prevent the chili from drying out. Remove the whole chipotle pepper.

Serve the chili topped with shredded cheese and a generous dollop of sour cream.

CHAPTER SEVEN
Grilling and Barbecuing

Over the many years that my family has been producing grassfed meats, grilling has become my year-round favorite way to prepare it. Searing steaks and burgers directly over the flames, then finishing them in the aura of the grill's heat perfumes them with a lovely smoky flavor while still allowing all that grassfed glory to shine through. For fancier occasions, I convert my grill to a smoker, and use the excuse of doing an authentic grassfed barbecue to hang out on my back porch for the better part of an afternoon, doing little more than reading a book, throwing a stick for the dog, and monitoring the smoker temperatures. I've become so convinced that the grill is essential for any grassfed cook that in 2005, I packed up my entire family and we flew to Argentina, where we spent a winter traveling around the country, learning their famous grassfed grilling techniques. Since most Americans don't have the means these days to construct a beautiful outdoor Argentine-style *parilla*, I've taken my lessons from South America and adapted them to American-style grills. The recipes you will see in this chapter reflect these lessons. But before we get going, let's clarify a few terms commonly used with outdoor cooking, and understand how they apply to your grassfed beef.

Grilling. Grilling is what happens when you create a hot fire and place a cut of meat directly over it for the entire cooking time. The typical cooking temperature can exceed 500°F. A popular method for cooking conventional, grain-fed steaks, it should be rarely used when cooking grassfed meat. As a general rule, forget about direct grilling with grassfed beef. The results of grilling grassfed beef at such temperatures can be disastrous: it is too easy to overcook it, and there will be a higher incidence of flare-ups. Furthermore, charred meats cooked fast, hot and well-done have been shown to contain two suspected carcinogens, polycyclic aromatic hydrocarbons (PAHs) and heterocyclic amines (HCAs). Ideally, to avoid these potential hazards, meat should be cooked at low temperatures and it should not be well-done—a happy coincidence, since this is the way that grassfed meat tastes best.

Indirect Grilling. With indirect grilling, the heat source is kept to one side of the grill surface. The meat is *briefly* seared directly over the flame, then moved away from the heat and allowed to come up to temperature on the side of the grill that is not lit. To generate flavorful smoke, presoaked wood chips can be added, or they can be left out to create a less complicated taste comparable to oven roasting. The temperature inside the cooking chamber is often between 350–450° F, but can be cooler. I'm a big advocate of indirect grilling; steaks are less likely to get dried out and overdone. It is also a good method for cooking roasts, but I find spit-roasting to be an even better method.

Spit-Roasting. Spit-roasting must be one of the most underrated outdoor cooking methods in this country. During the summer months, people cruise their farmers' markets seeking steaks, chops, chicken parts and the occasional pork shoulder or spare rib for an old-fashioned smoke, but many folks overlook all the other splendid cuts of meat that can be cooked outdoors on a spit, relegating these cuts to wintertime oven-roasting. This is a pity, because these are some of the best meats you can turn out on a grill—sirloin and sirloin tip roasts are browned on the outside and pink in the centers, and they glisten as they turn on the spit, ultimately yielding succulent feasts. For less than $150, most companies offer rotisserie attachments for their grills, greatly expanding the variety of meat you can cook. I cannot emphasize enough how wonderful these gadgets are, particularly for grassfed meats. Rotisseries keep the meat well away from the flame, allow it to baste in its juices, and enable a slow, controlled cook unlike any other outdoor method. Further, if you want to do a cookout and own a rotisserie, you can prepare the far less expensive cuts—the whole roasts—rather than shelling out big bucks for more expensive grill cuts, like Porterhouse steaks. You'll likely find that a rotisserie attachment will quickly pay for itself, both in savings from buying less-expensive meats, and by fool-proofing your grilling, providing you with perfectly cooked meats every time you cook outdoors.

Barbecue. Yum. Real barbecue was *made* for grassfed meat. Different from grilling, true barbecue is all about slow cooking with smoke. The heat source is indirect and cool, never rising above 250°F. Barbecue is ideal for cooking meats like chuck roasts and briskets, as the slow moist heat breaks down tough connective tissues, called collagen, making these cuts juicy and tender.

Authentic barbecue often uses "pits," Willy Wonka-esque cookers where the cool fire smolders in a firebox separate from the cooking chamber. But you don't have to buy an elaborate barbecue pit to enjoy good barbecue. Using a method similar to indirect grilling, a low fire can be maintained on one side of your charcoal kettle or gas grill, with the meat placed on the opposite side. Soaked wood chips such as hickory, apple or mesquite are placed on the fire to generate smoke. If using a charcoal grill, the lid is set so that the vents open above the meat, drawing the smoke across the grill and through the roast, giving it the same luscious flavor that comes from a barbecue pit.

A NOTE ON GAUGING GRILL TEMPS

Once the lid of your grill is closed for indirect cooking or barbecue, you can monitor the temperature of the cooking chamber with a grill or smoker thermometer, much like an oven thermometer. However, many recipes start by using that direct flame, which is harder to gauge. Gas grills have dials that read "low," "medium" and "high" to give you an idea of flame intensity but, just like oven thermostats, they aren't especially precise. Whether you're using a charcoal or gas grill, the easiest way to gauge flame intensity is by the hand test. Holding your hand five inches above the grill surface, count the number of seconds you can leave it there before you have to pull away. A cool flame will be 6–8 seconds; medium will be 5 seconds, and hot will be 2–3 seconds. Remember: it's a temperature test, not a macho test!

The Best Steak, Cooked Outdoors

1–2 tablespoons coarse salt

2–3 teaspoons ground black pepper

1–2 cloves garlic, minced

1 sirloin, sirloin tip, tri-tip, top round or London broil steak; OR 2 shoulder top blade, shoulder petite tender, rib, porterhouse, t-bone, top loin (NY strip), or tenderloin (filet mignon) steaks, cut 1¼- to 1½-inches thick.

The more experience I gain cooking steak, the more opinionated I've become about limiting seasonings to salt, pepper and garlic. There is too much glorious flavor in beef to justify corrupting it with excessive seasonings. However, if you would prefer to do something more glamorous, select any of the spice rubs, pastes or marinades from chapter 8, and experiment.

Combine the salt, pepper and garlic in a small bowl. Rub the mixture into both sides of the meat, then allow it to come to room temperature. Start the grill and warm it until it is hot. If you are using a gas grill, turn off all but one of the burners once it has come up to temperature. If you are using charcoal, be sure all the coals have been raked to one side. Use the hand test: the grate will be hot enough when you can hold your palm 3–4 inches above the metal grate for no more than three or four seconds.

Sear the steaks for 2 minutes on each side over direct heat. Move the steaks off direct heat, close the lid, and allow the steaks to cook over indirect heat, without turning, until they reach 120–135 degrees, about 5–7 minutes per pound.

Once they are cooked, remove the steaks to a platter and allow them to rest 5 minutes before serving.

Grilled Steaks in a Cilantro–Olive Paste

SERVES 2-4 (If steaks are boneless, allow ½ pound per person. For bone-in steaks, allow 1 pound per person.)

½ cup fresh cilantro

3 ounces pitted black olives

1 teaspoon coarse salt

½ teaspoon freshly ground black pepper

2 tablespoons olive oil

1 clove garlic

Either 1 sirloin, sirloin tip, tri-tip, top round or London broil steak; OR 2 shoulder top blade, shoulder petite tender, rib, porterhouse, T-bone, top loin (NY strip), tenderloin (filet mignon) steaks. The steak you choose should be about 1 ½ inches thick

These seasonings sound showy but, in truth, they perform as subtle accents, highlighting the full-beef flavor of the steaks. And while they are perfectly elegant fare, my kids love to gnaw on the bones and taste the black olives in the seasoning.

Add the first six ingredients to a food processor and purée, making a paste. Generously coat the steaks and allow them to come to room temperature.

Start the grill and warm it until it is medium–hot. If you are using a gas grill, turn off all but one of the burners once it has come up to temperature. If you are using charcoal, be sure all the coals have been raked to one side. Using the hand test, the grate will be hot enough when you can hold your palm five inches above it for no more than three seconds.

Sear the steaks for 2 minutes on each side directly over the flame. Then, move steaks to the part of the grill that is not lit. Set the lid in place and allow the steaks to cook, without flipping them, until they reach 120-140°F, about 15-25 minutes, depending on the size of the steak. Remove the steaks to a platter and tent loosely with foil, allowing the juices to redistribute in the meat before serving.

Sirloin Tip Marinated in Tamarind and Apple Butter

SERVES 3-4

1 teaspoon tamarind paste

2 tablespoons apple butter

2 tablespoons freshly grated ginger

¼ cup olive oil

2 cloves crushed garlic

2 teaspoons salt

3 tablespoons cider vinegar

½ teaspoon cayenne pepper

½ small onion, finely chopped

1 sirloin tip steak or London broil,
  1½-2 pounds

Sirloin tip steaks, as their name suggests, come from the end of the sirloin. They are not as tender as sirloin steaks and, like London broils, work beautifully with marinades. This is a wonderful steak to use if you are serving guests and don't have a lot of money to spend. There is very little waste with a sirloin tip, and often 1 steak can serve 3-4 people. Be sure to cut it across the grain, just as you would a London broil, to enjoy maximum tenderness. One note—if you don't have enough time to marinate the meat, this recipe also tastes great if you apply the marinade as a seasoning paste and then cook it immediately.

Tamarind paste, a seasoning used often in Indian cooking, can be found in most specialty food and large grocery stores.

Whisk together the first 9 ingredients, then pour into a baking pan or plastic zip-lock bag. Add the steak and thoroughly coat it with the marinade, cover, refrigerate, and allow it to marinate several hours or overnight. Before cooking, remove it from the refrigerator, blot the steak dry, and allow it to come to room temperature before you start your grill.

Start the grill and warm it until it is medium-hot. If you are using a gas grill, turn off all but one of the burners once it has come up to temperature. If you are using charcoal, be sure all the coals have been raked to one side. Using the hand test, the grate will be hot enough when you can hold your palm five inches above it for no more than three seconds.

Sear the steaks for 2 minutes on each side directly over the flame, then move them to the part of the grill that is not lit. Set the lid in place and allow the steaks to cook, without flipping them, until they reach 120–140°F, about 20–30 minutes. Remove the meat to a platter and tent loosely with foil, allowing the meat to rest five minutes before serving (the temperature will come up a few more degrees during this time).

Peanut–Crusted London Broil or Sirloin Tip Steak

ADVANCE PREPARATION REQUIRED

SERVES 4

1 recipe Green Pepper and Garlic Marinade (see Chapter 8).

2 pounds sirloin tip or London broil steak

1 cup chopped unsalted oil-roasted peanuts

London broils and sirloin tip steaks are great "family" steaks. They are less expensive and, because they contain a bit more connective tissue, they'll stand up well to marinades and fun seasonings, such as this twist on West African culinary tradition. If these particular seasonings aren't your thing, the technique described below will work with any of the beef marinades listed in Chapter 8.

Pour the marinade into a glass baking dish, large zipper-locking plastic bag, or a non-reactive bowl. Add the steak and turn thoroughly to coat. Cover, refrigerate, and allow it to marinate several hours or overnight, turning occasionally. Before cooking, remove it from the refrigerator, blot the steak dry, then roll it in the chopped peanuts. Allow the meat to come to room temperature before you start your grill.

Start the grill and warm one side only until it is medium-hot. Using the hand test, the grate will be hot enough when you can hold your palm 5 inches above it on the hot side for no more than 4 seconds.

Sear the steaks for 2 minutes per side over direct heat, then move them off the heat, close the lid, and cook, without turning, until they reach 120–140 degrees, about 5–7 minutes per pound (rarer meat will be more tender and juicy). Remove the meat to a platter and let rest 5 minutes before carving into thin slices along the diagonal (across the grain).

Steak Fajita Salad

SERVES 4

½ cup lime juice

½ cup tequila

4 tablespoons olive oil

2 pounds skirt, flank or flat-iron steak

3 medium yellow or white onions, peeled and sliced lengthwise, with root left intact

2 teaspoons balsamic vinegar

2 teaspoons coarse salt

2 teaspoons ground black pepper

4 cups field greens

1 cup chopped fresh cilantro

3 avocados, peeled and sliced

2 medium sweet red peppers, sliced into julienned strips

4 medium tomatoes

Special equipment: grill basket

Here's a cool dish for a hot summer night that would pair well with a margarita or just a glass of chilled kombucha.

Whisk together the lime juice, tequila, and 3 tablespoons of oil. Pour the marinade into a nonreactive dish, then add the steaks. Marinate 1–2 hours, turning periodically to keep evenly coated.

Heat one side of the grill until you can hold your hand 5 inches above the grate for no more than 3 seconds.

Brush the onions with olive oil, then place them in the grill basket. Grill over direct heat until tender, about 5 minutes per side. Remove the onions to a cutting board. Once they are cool enough to handle, remove the root ends and toss the slices with balsamic vinegar, salt and pepper.

Remove the steaks from the marinade and pat dry. Lay them directly over the flames. Sear the steaks over direct heat for 2 minutes per side. Move them off the heat, cover, and cook 4 minutes longer, or until it is done to your liking, remembering that skirt, flank and flat-iron steaks are best served rare.

Remove the steaks to a cutting board and let rest 5 minutes before carving. Slice ¼ inch thick diagonally across the grain. Arrange them on top of the field greens, along with the onions, cilantro, avocados, peppers and tomatoes. Dress with some olive oil and lemon or limejuice and a sprinkling of fine salt.

Coriander–Cinnamon Spiced Steak

SERVES 4

1 batch Coriander-Cinnamon Spice Rub (see Chapter 8)

2 pounds skirt, flank or flat-iron steak

Skirt and flank steaks are some of our most popular cuts for the serious beef eaters who like a little extra flavor and texture to their meat. Unfortunately, there are only 2 small steaks per beef animal. Thus, the lesser-known flat-iron, cut from the chuck primal, is a fantastic alternative for folks who like to exercise their canines on a high-flavor cut of meat.

Rub the spice rub all over the surface of the meat. Cover and refrigerate overnight. When you are ready to cook them, remove the steaks from the refrigerator and allow them to come to room temperature while you heat one side of the grill until you can hold your hand 5 inches above the grate for no more than 3 seconds.

Sear the steaks over direct heat for 2 minutes per side. Move them off direct heat, cover, and cook 4–8 minutes longer, or until it is done to your liking, remembering that skirt, flank and flat-iron steaks are best served rare. *Skirt steaks will take less indirect cooking time, as they are thinner (usually less than 1 inch thick). Flat irons, which are typically thicker (usually thicker than 1 inch), will take more time.*

Grilled Burgers

SERVES 4

1½ pounds ground beef

1¼ teaspoons fine salt

1¼ teaspoons ground black pepper

Cooking oil

For years I frittered around trying to make the perfect burger. I added garlic, Worcestershire sauce, bread crumb, egg, oyster sauce . . . any number of ingredients. Over time I discovered that, because ground beef is made from the most flavorful meat on the animal, less is more. A tiny bit of salt and a dash of pepper is all you need. Much of the flavor is built up by the sear on the grill, and then the prolonged indirect cooking time, which allows the natural sugars to caramelize over the surface of the meat. We like these burgers so much we eat them plain, as though they were fine steak—no ketchup, no mustard. We revel in the full, glorious, mineral-rich intense beef flavor all on its own.

Combine the ground beef with the salt and pepper. Loosely shape the meat into four balls. Gently flatten them until they are about 1 inch thick. With your fingertips, make a small well in the top of each patty to prevent the meat from getting puffy over the flames. Set the patties aside while you light one side of your grill and clean off the cooking grate with a wire brush.

When one side of the grill is medium–hot and you can hold your hand five inches above it for no more than four seconds, brush it down lightly with oil, then set the patties directly over the flame. Cover and cook 4 minutes per side. Move the burgers off the coals to indirect heat, cover, and cook 10 minutes longer.

ASADO: GRILLING ARGENTINE-STYLE

Asado has two meanings in Argentina. It is their Spanish word for "grill," but also describes slow-roasted beef short ribs which, according to most Argentineans you speak with, epitomizes the glory of Argentina's ember-roasted offerings. Short ribs are often overlooked here in the United States during grill season. We tend to think of them as "tough cuts," useful only for braises and stews during the winter months. In fact, short ribs had been so rarely purchased by our customers in the past that we'd been known to occasionally use them as dog food . . . until we traveled down to Argentina and learned just how scrumptious they are. It is true that you might have to chew this meat, and most Americans, I've noticed, have a quirky aversion to this notion. But if you roast short ribs on your rotisserie slowly for a minimum of two hours (three is even better if you can monitor the heat and keep it low enough), then season them with *salmuera* and set the table with a good set of steak knives, I *guarantee* you will not be disappointed. If you love grill flavor on your meat, if you like the sweetest perfume of smoke, and relish a deep beefy essence, I think you will join the Argentineans in favoring this cut over any steak or burger. In my estimation, nothing else compares. The consequence, however, is that all the hard-working dogs at Sap Bush Hollow are now rather resentful.

NOTE: In Argentina a classic *asado* is a long strip of short ribs, cut flanken-style, which can be roasted on a *parilla* (a special Argentine-style grill), then cut into individual ribs just before serving. If you have a butcher who will cut them flanken-style, so much the better. However, typically the short ribs in America are cut apart by the butcher. If that's the only way you can buy them, don't worry. Simply spear the meat on your rotisserie as you would kebabs on a skewer, and get grilling. To be faithful to my grilling instructors below the equator, I must admit that we did not use rotisseries to cook *asados* in Argentina, although they are used in neighboring countries.

Asado (GRILLED SHORT RIBS)

SERVES 5–6

1 batch *salmuera* (recipe follows)

5–6 pounds short ribs, bone-in (allow one pound of ribs per person)

If using a charcoal grill, light the coals and allow them to burn until they are covered with a layer of gray ash. Pour a line of coals down the left and right side of the grill, and place a drip pan or cast-iron skillet in the center. If cooking with gas, light the front and back burners only. Put your rotisserie attachment in place, spear the meat on the spit (if the ribs are flanken style, thread the spit between every second or third rib, zig-zag). Allow the meat to turn on the spit and slowly roast for 2–3 hours, until the tissue along the exterior of the bones begins to pull away and the meat, when sliced, appears nearly well-done throughout (although there should still be ample juices). As you cook the meat, be sure to leave the lid of the grill open. You want to be sure that the temperature *at the spit*, where the meat is, remains around 300 degrees. To gauge this, you should be able to hold your hand right next to the rotating meat for eight seconds.

Ten minutes before you serve the ribs, splash them liberally with the *salmuera*. Allow them to continue to turn on the rotisserie so that a salty crust forms. When you serve the meat, pass the *salmuera* bottle separately so your guests can add additional sauce as desired.

If you don't have a rotisserie: Heat the grill until it is about 300 degrees *at the grate*. This means you should be able to hold your hand just above the metal, almost touching it, for 8 seconds. Set the unseasoned meat bone-side down directly over the flames and allow the meat to roast, uncovered, for about three hours, or until the tissue begins to pull away from the bones and the meat, when sliced, appears nearly well-done throughout. There should still be plenty of juice when you slice it.

During this period, if using charcoal, you will need to pay close attention and add a few coals every few minutes to maintain the grill temperature. Do not flip the short ribs during the initial cooking time. The objective when cooking with this method is to allow the heated *bones,* and not the flames, to gently cook the meat.

Ten minutes before serving, splash the ribs liberally with *salmuera* and allow the meat to continue to cook while the salty crust forms, turning it to be sure the salt solution crusts over all sides. When you serve the meat, pass the *salmuera* separately so your guests can add additional seasoning to taste.

Salmuera ARGENTINA (AND BRAZIL'S) SALT-SATURATED GARLIC WATER

5–6 cloves garlic, finely sliced

1 tablespoon black peppercorns, coarsely crushed using mortar and pestle

1 tablespoon white peppercorns, coarsely crushed using mortar and pestle

7 tablespoons coarse salt, plus extra

1 clean, empty 750 ml wine bottle and cork or stopper

Here you have an unbelievably inexpensive and flavorful seasoning for grassfed beef. Sure, herby stuff is nice, and spicy stuff is fun. But when you have great flavored beef, this is all you need. This is the one seasoning that should be applied near the end of cooking. Drizzle it over your meat liberally a few minutes before it comes off the grill, then flip your cuts around so that the heat will encrust the salt water onto the meat. Once you've tried it on your short ribs, try it on steaks, chicken, pork or lamb.

Combine the garlic, black and white peppercorns and 2 tablespoons salt in a medium-sized saucepan. Pour in three cups water, then bring the mixture to a rolling boil for 30 seconds. Turn the heat off and allow it to cool for 5 minutes.

Using a funnel, add 3 tablespoons salt to the bottom of the wine bottle. Then pour in the garlic water, including the sliced garlic and ground peppercorns. Cork the bottle. Using your thumb to hold the cork in place, shake vigorously until all the salt is incorporated into the water. Add 2 more tablespoons salt and shake again. If all this salt is absorbed and none has collected on the bottom of the bottle, add additional salt. In a good *salmuera*, the water must be *completely* saturated with salt. This means you must continue to add salt and shake until the water will absorb no more and a small pile of salt has gathered on the bottom of the bottle.

Shave off the corner of the cork to allow the mixture to be easily drizzled (we use a pour-spout stopper), then store at room temperature for up to three months, adding more salt, pepper, garlic and hot water to taste to enrich the flavor after each use.

Before applying to the meat, place your bottle of *salmuera* on the grate of your grill to heat up. For maximum flavor and efficient cooking, always be sure your *salmuera* is hot before you use it. Once you've splashed it on the meat on your grill, be sure to set the *salmuera* on the table so that your guests can add more to their meat to taste.

Short Ribs Marinated in Cayenne and Garlic

SERVES 3–5

4 cloves garlic

1 tablespoon cayenne pepper

1 small onion, peeled and cut in half

1 tablespoon coarse salt

1 tablespoon white peppercorns, coarsely ground

1 tablespoon black peppercorns, coarsely ground

4 tablespoons cognac

4 tablespoons olive oil

4 tablespoons red wine vinegar

4 bay leaves

4 sprigs fresh rosemary

3–5 pounds short ribs

On rare occasions, for variation, Argentineans will marinate their short ribs before cooking an asado. This recipe comes from the Gomez family, who hosted Bob, Saoirse and me during our travels. It is wonderfully fragrant, and not nearly as spicy as you might imagine with all that cayenne pepper!

Add the garlic, cayenne, onion, salt, peppercorns, cognac, olive oil and vinegar to the large bowl of a food processor. Purée to make a paste. Rub the paste into the meat, then set the ribs in a plastic bag. Set the bay leaves and rosemary on top, then seal the bag tightly and refrigerate several hours or overnight.

When you are ready to grill, remove the ribs from the bag, but do not blot off the paste. Allow the meat to come to room temperature, then grill as directed in the *asado* recipe above.

SALSA CRIOLLA AND CHIMICHURRI

Whenever Argentina is a chosen subject for foodie magazines, *salsa criolla* and *chimichurri* are touted as the quintessential seasonings of the nation, synonymous with the country's famous grassfed beef. However, the more *asadores* and grill fanatics we interviewed, and the deeper we traveled into the country feasting on *asados* in the homes of beef-loving families (rather than in tourist restaurants), the less we saw of these sauces.

While the great *asadores* occasionally serve these sauces for a little variation, when we dined in restaurants, we found that *salsa criolla* and *chimichurri* appeared in abundance on the tables where the meat being served was either poorly prepared or slightly rancid. In short, the sauces seemed to be used either to placate tourists or to mask not-so-good beef. Still, they are tasty, and I'd be remiss if, after spending so much time in Argentina, I failed to give these recipes. These two versions have been handed down for generations in the Gomez family and make splashy accompaniments. If you are preparing grilled steaks or an *asado*, consider using these condiments on the meat very lightly—and then having some good tortilla chips on the table to really enjoy their flavor.

Salsa Criolla

1 red bell pepper, finely diced

1 green bell pepper, finely diced

2 fresh tomatoes, finely diced

1 large onion, finely diced

2 tablespoons red wine vinegar

3 tablespoons olive oil

1 tablespoon Hungarian paprika

2 cloves garlic, minced

salt and pepper

Combine the bell peppers, tomatoes and onion in a porcelain, stainless steel or other non-reactive bowl. Mix well, then season to taste with salt and pepper. Stir in the vinegar, oil, paprika and garlic. Serve immediately, or refrigerate for an hour while the flavors blend.

Chimichurri

1 cup water

½ cup red wine vinegar

2 tablespoons fresh oregano, chopped

2 tablespoons fresh parsley, chopped

2 tablespoons fresh thyme, chopped

4 cloves garlic, minced

½ teaspoon salt

½ teaspoon ground black pepper

1 cup olive oil

2 bay leaves

Occasionally, some folks in Argentina use chimichurri *as a marinade for their* asados, *although this is not a very common practice. Most often it is served on the side as a condiment, to be used very sparingly.*

Whisk together the water, vinegar, oregano, parsley, thyme, garlic, salt and pepper. Slowly add the oil, whisking continuously as you pour. Add the bay leaves, stir briefly, then allow the mixture to rest a minimum of 30 minutes before serving, allowing the flavors to incorporate.

Beef Kebabs

ADVANCE PREPARATION REQUIRED

SERVES 4–6

1 recipe Garlic-Lime Marinade,
    OR Dad's Tamari-Balsamic Marinade,
    OR Cayenne Garlic Marinade,
    OR Tamari Orange Whiskey Marinade
    (see Chapter 8).

2 pounds beef cut for kebabs
    (alternatively, use a London broil,
    sirloin tip, or sirloin steak cut into
    1½-inch cubes)

Metal skewers, or bamboo skewers
    soaked in water for 30 minutes

Kebabs, when marinated in advance, are a terrific way to create a fast, tasty meal. I find that the secret to enjoying them lies in appreciating the fact that they come from slightly chewier cuts of meat—not so chewy as to warrant stewing, but just chewy enough to enjoy a lusty pull with your teeth as the rare meat releases juices on your tongue. If a few extra hungry souls show up at your table, expand the food available by skewering up and grilling some onions, peppers, tomatoes or summer squash to go with it.

Pour the marinade into a large, stainless-steel, porcelain, glass, or other nonreactive bowl. Add the beef and mix well to coat. Cover and refrigerate overnight or for a minimum of 2 hours. Stir them periodically to ensure all parts of the meat have an opportunity to absorb the marinade.

When you are ready to grill, remove the meat from the marinade, blot dry with a paper towel, thread it on skewers, and allow it to come to room temperature while you prepare the grill.

Heat one side of the grill until the flame is medium-hot. You should be able to hold your hand five inches beyond the flame for no more than 4 seconds. Scrape the grate clean with a wire brush, then brush it lightly with oil.

Grill over direct heat, covered, for 2 minutes. Turn the skewers, and grill 2 minutes longer, still covered. Move them off the heat, cover, and cook over indirect heat for 5 minutes longer for medium-rare meat. Serve immediately.

Brisket and Suds

SERVES 6-12 (allow ½ pound of meat per person)

1 batch Texas Style Spice Rub

1 batch Share-the-Beer Marinade

1 batch Sweet Tomato Barbecue Sauce

(all of these recipes appear in Chapter 8)

1 piece flat-cut brisket, 3–6 lbs (NOTE: If you wish to do an entire brisket, which is considerably larger than 3–6 pounds, be sure to double the amount of spice rub and marinade you make.)

7 cups mesquite or hickory wood chips or chunks, soaked in water. (NOTE: if you are using a gas grill, use only wood chips, not chunks. You will only need about 2 cups of wood chips in this case.)

Your main job when cooking a brisket is to convert the waxy connective tissue, called collagen, to gelatin, making the meat tender. To accomplish this, it helps to incorporate some moisture into your cooking and to let the internal temperature of the meat slowly rise to over 200 degrees. Cooking a brisket can take hours; if you have a big piece of meat, it can take all day. Of course, such a task offers a prime opportunity to nurse beers (organic, local brews, of course) and avoid chores. However, if you aren't up for a full-day project, then smoke the brisket per the instructions below, but only for two hours. After that, wrap the meat in foil (or set it in an ovenproof casserole with a tight-fitting lid) and roast it in a 300-degree oven until it is fork tender. (This still might take another three hours if you are working with a large piece of brisket.)

The day before you plan to feast, combine the ingredients for the Texas Style Spice Rub and set aside. Whisk together the ingredients for the Share-the-Beer Marinade, reserve one cup, then pour the remainder into a glass, porcelain or stainless-steel bowl. Add the brisket, turn it well to coat, and cover it tightly. Allow the meat to marinate overnight.

On feast day (early in the day), remove the brisket from the marinade and pat it dry. Massage a generous portion of the spice rub into the meat and allow it to come to room temperature. Pour the wood chunks or chips into a bucket of cold water and allow them to soak for a minimum of 30 minutes (ideally longer).

If using charcoal, light your grill, keeping the fire on only one side, and allow it to heat until the cooking chamber is about 200 degrees (a smoking thermometer will be of great help here). Toss a handful of the soaked wood chips or chunks directly on the coals.

If using a gas grill, light the grill, turn all burners to high, then put the soaked wood chips in a foil tray and set it down directly over one burner. Close the lid and preheat the cooking chamber (all burners still on high) until smoke billows out. Turn off all but the one burner beneath the wood chips and allow the cooking chamber to come down to 200 degrees (if the chamber won't cool down that low, get it as cool as you can, then plan for a shorter cook time).

Set the brisket in a cast iron skillet or foil roasting pan and put it on the cool side of the grill. Cover. If using a charcoal grill, open the lid vents and arrange the cover so the vents are directly over the meat—this draws the smoke across the meat.

Barbecue for roughly 1 hour and 10 minutes per pound of meat, basting each hour with the reserved marinade (your cooking time might be less if your gas grill maintains your cooking chamber higher than 200 degrees). On a charcoal grill, the cooking chamber temperature will fluctuate as you burn coals and add more. Be sure never to let the temperature fall below 140 degrees, to safeguard against botulism. Add charcoal as necessary to maintain heat, and wood chips or chunks to maintain smoke. If using a gas grill, be sure you start with ample propane and monitor the gas flow as your thermometer warrants. The meat will be ready when it is fork-tender. Remove it to a platter, carve across the grain and serve with the Sweet Tomato Barbecue Sauce.

Rosemary Studded Spit-Roasted Beef

SERVES 6–8

¼ cup fresh rosemary leaves

3 cloves garlic, slivered

2 tablespoons coarse salt

1 tablespoon ground black pepper

1 round roast (top, bottom or eye round), or sirloin roast, approximately 3-4 pounds

1 recipe horseradish cream (optional) (recipe appears in Chapter 4)

Don't pass over those beautiful beef roasts on display at your farmers' market just because it's summer. If you're looking to create a great grilled-beef experience for a crowd, without a lot of expense, this makes a lovely, elegant feast, especially if you serve it with a horseradish cream sauce. I like this roast best off the rotisserie, but you can also prepare it using the indirect cooking method.

Cut a series of ½-inch-deep holes all over the surface of the meat, each about 2 inches apart. If there is a layer of fat, be sure the cut is deep enough to reach the muscle tissue beneath it. Insert the fresh rosemary leaves and a sliver of garlic in each hole, then rub the salt and pepper all over the roast.

If using the indirect cooking method, heat one side of the grill with the lid down until the chamber is about 200 degrees. If using a rotisserie on a gas grill, preheat the grill by using the front and rear burners. If using a rotisserie on a charcoal grill, light the coals and then rake them into two rows, leaving a gap down the center. Be sure to place a drip pan under the meat if using a rotisserie. Regardless of your method, cook the meat with the grill lid down.

Monitor the temperature of the cooking chamber, being sure to add more coals or adjust the flame to keep the temperature between 200 and 250 degrees. The internal temperature of the finished meat should be 125 degrees for medium-rare. Estimated cooking time will be approximately 40 minutes per pound. To serve, carve the meat very thinly and, if you like, offer horseradish cream sauce.

NOTE: Sometimes grills and circumstances are uncooperative in allowing you to keep the temperature of the cooking chamber cool enough, particularly with the lid down. Since you are not trying to smoke the meat, in this instance, it is fine to remove the lid if you are using a rotisserie. If you are using the indirect method, get the chamber as close to the ideal temp as you can, then carefully monitor the internal temperature of the meat and the chamber. If necessary, you can periodically remove the grill lid for a few moments if there is too much heat build-up.

Java-Cinnamon Smoked Chuck Roast

SERVES 6–8

1 batch Java-Cinnamon Spice Rub (see Chapter 8)

1 batch Coffee Molasses Mop (see Chapter 8)

1 boneless chuck eye roast (or other boneless chuck roast), 3–4 pounds

7 cups maple or hickory wood chips or chunks, soaked in water.

(NOTE: If you are using a gas grill, use only wood chips, not chunks. You will only need about 2 cups of wood chips in this case.)

If you like to linger around your barbecue even as the days grow short, here's one last thrill for the grill that tastes great as summer wanes and the flavors of fall start to tempt your palate.

The day before you plan to cook your roast, massage all but ¼ cup of the Java-Cinnamon Spice Rub into the meat. Wrap it in plastic and refrigerate overnight. About 8 or 9 hours before you are ready to eat, remove the meat and allow it to come to room temperature. Meanwhile, prepare the Coffee Molasses Mop per the directions below, then prepare your grill.

If using charcoal, light your grill, keeping the fire on only one side, and allow it to heat until the cooking chamber is about 200 degrees (a smoking thermometer will be of great help here). Toss a handful of the soaked wood chips or chunks directly on the coals.

If using a gas grill, light the grill, turn all burners to high, then put all the soaked wood chips in a foil tray and set it down directly over one burner. Close the lid and preheat the cooking chamber (all burners still on high) until smoke billows out. Turn off all but the one burner beneath the wood chips and allow the cooking chamber to come down to 200 degrees (if the chamber won't cool that low, get it as cool as you can and plan for a shorter cook time).

Place the chuck roast in a large cast-iron skillet (or disposable roasting pan) on the side opposite the fire. Close the grill lid. If you are using a charcoal grill, arrange the lid so that the vents are partially open and on the same side as the meat in order to draw the smoke through. Monitor the temperature of the smoking chamber throughout the day, making sure it stays around 200 degrees. (If you are using a charcoal barbecue, you will occasionally have to add more coals to maintain the fire, and wood chips or chunks to maintain the smoke. For safety, be sure the cooking chamber never falls below 140 degrees.)

Allow the roast to smoke for about four hours, being sure to baste it with the Coffee Molasses Mop every time you lift the grill lid. Then, make the fire hotter, allowing the cooking chamber to come up to 400 degrees. Pour any remaining mop into the bottom of the pan, cover it with aluminum foil, put the grill lid back down, and allow the meat to cook an additional 3 hours, or until it is fork-tender (this finishing can also take place in the oven, if you'd rather, using a covered dish). Remove the roast from the heat and allow it to rest about 10 minutes, loosely tented with the foil.

Carve the meat and arrange it on a platter, and serve the pan juices on the side.

99

Burgundy Chuck Roast

Serves 4-10

2 tablespoons coarse salt

2 teaspoons ground black pepper

4 cups burgundy or other dry red wine

1 onion, minced

2 cloves garlic, minced

¼ cup fresh parsley, coarsely chopped

1 tablespoon fresh thyme leaves

1 (2–5 pound) chuck eye roast, top round, bottom round or eye round.

Marinades are wonderful for what might otherwise be called "the tougher" cuts of meat, like chucks and rounds. Many people think this is because marinades tenderize the meat, but they don't. In fact, if left in a marinade for too long, the meat turns gray and mushy. The real reasons "the tougher cuts" fare so well with marinating is because they are less inclined to turn mushy and they have more robust flavor, which means the great beefy taste will shine through even if your marinade seasonings penetrate deeply through the meat. Like the Rosemary-Studded Beef, this dish also pairs well with horseradish cream sauce (recipe appears in Chapter 4).

Press the salt and pepper into the surface of the beef. Set aside. Combine the wine, onion, garlic, parsley and thyme in a glass, porcelain or stainless-steel bowl. Mix well. Add the beef and turn it until it is well moistened. Allow the meat to bathe in the marinade for 6 hours at room temperature, or overnight in the refrigerator, being sure to turn it occasionally.

Start a medium-sized fire in your grill. If using a rotisserie, rake the coals (or light the gas burners) on either side of where the spit will turn. If using the indirect method, light only one side of the grill. Cover the grill and allow the cooking chamber to come up to about 250 degrees.

Remove the roast from the marinade and pat it dry. If using a rotisserie, slide the meat onto the spit and put it in place over the grate. If using the indirect method, set the meat on the side of the grill that is not lit. Keep the cooking chamber between 225 and 275 degrees, cooking about 1 hour per pound of meat, removing the meat when the internal temperature is between 125 and 140 degrees.

NOTE: Sometimes grills and circumstances are uncooperative in allowing you to keep the temperature of the cooking chamber cool enough, particularly with the lid down. Since you are not trying to smoke the meat, in this instance, it is fine to remove the lid if you are using a rotisserie. If you are using the indirect method, get the chamber as close to the ideal temp as you can, then carefully monitor the internal temperature of the meat and the chamber. If necessary, you can periodically remove the grill lid for a few moments if there is too much heat build-up.

CHAPTER EIGHT

Beef Seasonings: Rubs, Pastes and Marinades

The following recipes have been used throughout this book. Now that you've read through it and have become a grassfed beef master cook, I'll leave you with these seasoning blends. You can use them to make up your own grassfed beef recipes, as something that works great on a steak will also work well on a roast; a marinade for kebabs will also be delicious on a London broil. You can use what appears here to experiment, coming up with your own favorite grassfed beef recipes.

Rubs

CORIANDER-CINNAMON SPICE RUB

MAKES ABOUT ¼ CUP

2 teaspoons granulated garlic

2 teaspoons fine-ground unrefined (Celtic gray) sea salt

1 teaspoon ground black pepper

2 teaspoons paprika

2 teaspoons ground coriander

1 teaspoon ground cumin

1 teaspoon ground cinnamon

⅛ teaspoon ground cloves

GARAM MASALA

This spice blend is an essential ingredient in a number of Indian dishes. The recipe below is for the spice blend alone. If you wish to directly season meat with it, add 1 tablespoon of unrefined salt once you've ground the spices.

MAKES ABOUT ⅓ CUP

1 (5-inch) cinnamon stick, broken into pieces

6 black cardamom pods

8 green cardamom pods

1 teaspoon whole cloves

2 teaspoons whole cumin seeds

3 teaspoons whole black peppercorns

2 teaspoons whole fennel seeds

4 bay leaves, torn into pieces

Heat a skillet over a medium flame, then add all the ingredients. Dry roast the spices, stirring often, until they are lightly browned and fragrant. Store in an airtight container and grind just prior to using (I have a spare coffee grinder that I use just for spices so my coffee doesn't taste funny).

GARLIC SPICE RUB

If using fresh garlic, plan to use all of the rub immediately, or cover and refrigerate untouched portions and plan to use them within a few days. (The garlic will go sour in a few days).

MAKES ABOUT ¼ CUP

2 tablespoons coarse unrefined (Celtic gray) sea salt

1 tablespoon ground black pepper

1 tablespoon granulated garlic (or 3 cloves chopped fresh garlic)

MOROCCAN SPICE RUB

MAKES SLIGHTLY MORE THAN ¼ CUP

1 teaspoon ground ginger

1 tablespoon sweet paprika

2 teaspoons ground turmeric

1 teaspoon ground cumin

1 teaspoon ground coriander

1 tablespoon fine-ground unrefined (Celtic gray) sea salt

2 teaspoons ground black pepper

ROSEMARY AND THYME HERB RUB

MAKES ABOUT ⅓ CUP

2 tablespoons coarse sea salt

1 tablespoon ground black pepper

2 cloves garlic, minced

1 tablespoon crumbled dried rosemary

1 tablespoon crumbled dried thyme

ROSEMARY HERB RUB

MAKES ABOUT ½ CUP

2 tablespoons crumbled dried rosemary

1 tablespoon crumbled dried oregano

2 tablespoons coarse unrefined (Celtic gray) sea salt

1 tablespoon ground black pepper

4 cloves garlic, minced

TEXAS STYLE SPICE RUB

MAKES ABOUT ¾ CUP

2 tablespoons coarse salt

1 teaspoon ground cumin

3 tablespoons chili powder

2 teaspoons garlic powder

¼ cup turbinado, sucanat or other unrefined or partially refined sugar

½ teaspoon cayenne pepper (optional)

1 tablespoon ground black pepper

JAVA-CINNAMON SPICE RUB

MAKES ABOUT ⅔ CUP

2 tablespoons ground coffee

2 tablespoons chili powder

2 teaspoons ground black pepper

2 tablespoons coarse sea salt

2 tablespoons ground cinnamon

2 tablespoons granulated maple sugar (or sucanat, turbinado or other unrefined or partially refined sugar)

Pastes

For all the following recipes, combine the listed ingredients in the small bowl of a food processor and blend to a paste.

CARIBBEAN CHILI GARLIC PASTE

MAKES ABOUT 1⅓ CUPS

1 small onion, peeled and cut in half

3 cloves garlic, peeled

2 hot chilies, cut in half with seeds and white membrane removed

2 teaspoons crumbled dried thyme, or 2 tablespoons chopped fresh thyme

2 tablespoons sweet paprika

1 tablespoon coarse unrefined (Celtic gray) sea salt

½ cup olive oil

CORIANDER-HERB PASTE

MAKES A LITTLE MORE THAN ½ CUP

2 tablespoons coarse salt

1 tablespoon ground black pepper

1 tablespoon chopped fresh rosemary, or 1 teaspoon crumbled dried rosemary

1 tablespoon chopped fresh thyme, or 1 teaspoon crumbled dried thyme

1 teaspoon ground coriander

1 teaspoon ground fennel

¼ cup olive oil

GARLIC AND PARSLEY HERB PASTE

MAKES ABOUT ⅓ CUP

1 clove crushed, minced garlic

1 tablespoon coarse unrefined (Celtic gray) sea salt

2 teaspoons ground black pepper

4 tablespoons olive oil

1 tablespoon dried parsley

OREGANO-MUSTARD PASTE

MAKES ABOUT ¾ CUP

¼ cup olive oil

1 tablespoon crumbled dried oregano

2 cloves minced garlic

1 tablespoon Dijon mustard

1 tablespoon coarse salt

2 teaspoons ground black pepper

PEANUT-LIME PASTE

MAKES ABOUT 1 CUP

¼ cup natural peanut butter

3 tablespoons unsalted roasted peanuts

¼ cup chopped fresh cilantro

3 tablespoons lime juice

3 tablespoons water

1 tablespoon grated fresh ginger

1 small shallot, peeled

½ teaspoon ground coriander

½ teaspoon Tabasco or other hot sauce

½ teaspoon coarse salt

Marinades

BELL PEPPER AND GARLIC MARINADE

MAKES ABOUT 1½ CUPS

½ cup chopped onion

1 medium bell pepper, cored, seeded, and minced

4 cloves garlic, minced

½ teaspoon crushed red pepper

2 tablespoons grated fresh ginger

1 tablespoon coarse unrefined (Celtic gray) sea salt

2 teaspoons ground black pepper

¼ cup peanut or olive oil

DAD'S TAMARI-BALSAMIC MARINADE

MAKES ABOUT 1½ CUPS

½ cup olive oil

¼ cup tamari

½ cup Balsamic vinegar

2 cloves garlic, crushed

2 tablespoons honey

GARLIC-LIME MARINADE

MAKES SLIGHTLY MORE THAN 1 CUP

2 cloves garlic, crushed

2 teaspoons coarse unrefined (Celtic gray) sea salt

¼ teaspoon ground cumin

½ teaspoon ground black pepper

1 tablespoon dried parsley

½ cup lime juice

½ cup olive oil

PAPRIKA-LIME MARINADE

MAKES ABOUT ¾ CUP

½ cup lime juice

1½ tablespoons honey

½ teaspoon ground cumin

½ teaspoon sweet paprika

¼ teaspoon ground coriander

1 teaspoon coarse unrefined (Celtic gray) sea salt

½ teaspoon ground black pepper

½ teaspoon crumbled dried thyme

SHARE-THE-BEER MARINADE

MAKES ABOUT 4 ¼ CUPS

24 ounces beer

½ cup molasses

1-2 teaspoons Tabasco sauce

3 tablespoons Texas-Style Spice Rub, above

½ cup cider vinegar

TAMARIND APPLE BUTTER MARINADE

MAKES ABOUT ¾ CUP

1 teaspoon tamarind paste

2 tablespoons apple butter

2 tablespoons freshly grated ginger

¼ cup olive oil

2 cloves crushed garlic

2 teaspoons salt

3 tablespoons cider vinegar

½ teaspoon cayenne pepper

½ small onion, finely chopped

TEQUILA-LIME MARINADE

MAKES ABOUT 1⅓ CUPS

½ cup tequila

½ cup lime juice

3 tablespoons olive oil

THAI MARINADE

MAKES ABOUT 1½-2 CUPS

¼ cup Asian fish sauce

2 tablespoons tamari or soy sauce

3 tablespoons lime juice

3 tablespoons peanut oil

3 medium cloves of garlic, minced

1 tablespoon chopped lemon grass (optional)

¼ cup chopped fresh cilantro

1 tablespoon coarsely chopped fresh ginger (or 1 teaspoon ground dried ginger)

1 tablespoon honey

1 tablespoon sesame oil

1 teaspoon crushed red pepper

2 tablespoons coarsely chopped fresh chives

½ cup chopped onion

CAYENNE GARLIC MARINADE

MAKES ABOUT 1¼ CUPS

4 cloves garlic

1 tablespoon cayenne pepper

1 small onion, peeled and cut in half

1 tablespoon coarse salt

1 tablespoon white peppercorns, coarsely ground

1 tablespoon black peppercorns, coarsely ground

4 tablespoons cognac

4 tablespoons olive oil

4 tablespoons red wine vinegar

4 bay leaves

4 sprigs fresh rosemary

TAMARI ORANGE WHISKEY MARINADE

MAKES ABOUT 3 CUPS

1 cup orange juice

3 cloves garlic, minced

½ cup bourbon whiskey

¼ cup olive oil

3 tablespoons Dijon mustard

¼ cup honey

¼ cup tamari

¼ cup cider vinegar

½ medium onion, minced

1 tablespoon fresh ginger, minced

Barbecue Sauces

TAMARIND-GINGER BARBECUE SAUCE

MAKES SLIGHTLY MORE THAN 2 CUPS

2 cups meat broth, preferably homemade (see Meat Broth, Chapter 3)

½ cup honey

2 tablespoons grated fresh ginger

1 tablespoon chopped fresh parsley, or 1 teaspoon dried parsley

1 tablespoon chopped fresh chives, or 1 teaspoon dried chives

1 teaspoon spicy brown mustard

1 teaspoon ground cinnamon

¼ teaspoon ground cayenne pepper

1 clove garlic, minced

½ cup strong black coffee

1 tablespoon tamarind paste

Combine all the ingredients in a saucepan. Bring the mixture to a boil, then reduce the heat and allow the sauce to simmer until it is reduced by one-third.

APPLE-BOURBON BARBECUE SAUCE

MAKES 3½–4 CUPS SAUCE

½ cup butter

1 yellow or white medium onion, finely chopped

½ cup maple syrup

½ cup bourbon

½ cup cider vinegar

½ cup apple butter

¼ cup Dijon mustard

⅓ cup apple cider

Melt the butter in a saucepan over medium heat. Add the onion and sauté until translucent. Whisk in the remaining ingredients and allow the mixture to come to a boil for 30 seconds before reducing it to a simmer. Simmer for 30 minutes to thicken. Refrigerate leftovers in an airtight container.

SWEET TOMATO BARBECUE SAUCE

MAKES ABOUT 2 CUPS

1 tablespoon butter

1 medium onion, finely chopped

1 cup strong black coffee

3 cloves garlic, minced

½ cup honey

½ cup cider vinegar

4 tablespoons tomato paste

2 tablespoons honey mustard

1 teaspoon salt

1 teaspoon freshly ground black pepper

Melt the butter in a saucepan over a medi-um flame. Add the onions and sauté until translucent. Stir in the remaining ingredients and allow the sauce to simmer, uncovered, until lightly thickened, about 20 minutes. If desired, season to taste with additional honey, vinegar, salt and pepper. Serve warm. If refrigerated in an air-tight container, the sauce will keep several weeks.

COFFEE MOLASSES MOP

MAKES ABOUT 2½ CUPS

2 cups strong black coffee

¼ cup Java-Cinnamon Spice Rub (above)

½ cup molasses

1 cinnamon stick

Whisk together the coffee, spice rub and molasses in a medium saucepan on your stovetop. Add the cinnamon stick, turn the heat on to medium, and allow the mixture to come to a boil, stirring often. Reduce the heat to low and allow the mop to simmer for about 20 minutes.

Index

ABOUT THE AUTHOR

Shannon Hayes works with three generations of her family raising grassfed and pastured meats on Sap Bush Hollow Farm in Upstate New York. She is the author of several books, blogs daily at ShannonHayes.org and for *Yes!* Magazine. Hayes' quirky lifestyle, her attempts to live a life of personal accountability and sustainability, and her current research and writings about homemaking as an ecological movement have landed her and her family on the pages of the New York Times, Brain Child Magazine, Lancaster Farming, Small Farm Quarterly, Hobby Farm Home Magazine, The New York Times Magazine, The Atlantic, National Public Radio, Grit, The Katie Couric Show, *Yes!* Magazine, Elle Magazine, as well as the national newspapers of Germany, Turkey and Canada, the Arab News and the Pakistan Observer. Hayes holds a Ph.D. in sustainable agriculture and community development from Cornell University.